SCAM
school
ACADEMY

SCAM school ACADEMY

by **Brian Brushwood**

doodles + layout by Jon Tilton, Brandt Hughes

Advanced Lessons in Scoring Free Drinks,

Doing Magic

& Becoming the Life of the Party

Skyhorse Publishing

Skyhorse Publishing books may be purchased in bulk at special discounts for sales promotion, corporate gifts, fund-raising, or educational purposes. Special editions can also be created to specifications. For details, contact the Special Sales Department, Skyhorse Publishing, 307 West 36th Street, 11th Floor, New York, NY 10018 or info@ skyhorsepublishing.com.

Skyhorse® and Skyhorse Publishing® are registered trademarks of Skyhorse Publishing, Inc.®, a Delaware corporation.

Visit our website at www.skyhorsepublishing.com.

10 9 8 7 6 5 4 3
Library of Congress Cataloging-in-Publication Data is available on file.

Cover design by Brandt Hughes and Rain Saukas
Cover photos courtesy of the author

Print ISBN: 978-1-63220-656-5
Printed in China

CONTENTS

INTRODUCTION

Thank you.

Sincerely, you have absolutely no idea how much it means to us that you made *Scam School Academy* possible.

When we launched the original *Scam School* book, we honestly had no idea what to expect. We suspected that we were onto a good idea, and we certainly put a lot of hustle into the writing, drawings, video illustrations, and audio commentaries ... But until the day after launch, Jon and I didn't know if there was even going to be a sequel to the first book.

However, once the first book became the top selling magic book in the country, we knew we were on to something. We also knew that we wanted *Scam School Academy* to be even more ambitious.

One of the most satisfying aspects of *Scam School's* release has been receiving feedback on this exchange between Teller and me from 19 years ago. I was a 20-year-old kid starting out in magic, trying desperately to find my own voice, and Teller's fantastic essay is, without question, the reason I'm where I am today. If you haven't read it, I strongly encourage you to do so. Teller's wisdom will absolutely sharpen your magic presentation and inspire you to try for ever-greater things.

READ TELLER'S LETTER HERE

bit.ly/1DMXHSg

However, I've not previously given any advice as to how I implemented Teller's suggestions. Everyone's different, but here are a couple of the lessons I've learned in the last 19 years:

#1 - Don't wait. There are a million very good reasons why you should wait just a little bit longer before you start your next venture . . . Ignore all of them.

Don't wait to get started. Don't wait to pick up the phone. Don't wait to start writing new material. Say "Yes" and "Immediately" often.

You're going to find eight million excuses on why you should wait. You should wait for them to call you back. You should wait until you buy better props. You should wait until you can hire a professional photographer. Wait until your new routine is ready. Wait until know-nothing doofuses who happen to have started their careers before you write you back with sage words of wisdom (that's me I'm talking about).

Don't. Wait.

The only thing separating you from having your best show possible is 10,000 hours of live performances. And while that sounds like an unfair, daunting amount of time and effort to put into becoming great, keep this in mind: *the time is going to pass anyway*. You can either spend it working towards your goal, or waiting.

Whatever's wrong with your show, it's nothing that a thousand performances won't fix. So get out there now and start performing.

#2 – Find a safe place to be bad, so you can become good.

Failure is an integral part of success, so figure out where you can safely be bad immediately.

For me, it meant performing on 6th street and getting chased off by the cops. I could get six performances under my belt in one night, and I didn't have to ask anyone for the booking. The audiences gave me instant (and painfully honest) feedback, and occasionally I'd come home with 50 bucks in my pocket.

Before I started Scam School, I spent a year putting together travel videos of life on the road at www.shwood.com/bbotr. They weren't great (and nobody watched them), but it taught me how to tell stories and host in front of the camera.

Once Scam School became popular, I realized that I had zero experience keeping a live broadcast interesting . . . So I started doing the BBLiveShow, the "Best Worst Show on the Internet." Nobody paid me to do it, but we developed a very small audience and had a lot of fun . . . and the experience was absolutely vital to creating Night Attack, winner of both "Best Video Podcast" and "Best Mature Podcast" at the 2015 Podcast Awards . . . which led to two Billboard #1 Comedy Albums.

My point is, no matter where you are, you've got more to learn. Don't just be unafraid to be bad . . . find the right venue to be aggressively, fearlessly bad so you can figure out how to become good. And that goes for whether you want to become a professional magician, an entertainer, or simply the life of the party.

About

BRIAN

Since 2000, Brian Brushwood has been touring nationally and internationally with his "Bizarre Magic Show" ... a thrill-ride mashup of dangerous stunts, fire-eating, mind-reading, and comedy magic. He's appeared twice on the Tonight Show with Jay Leno, as well as dozens of national TV programs nationwide. He's headlined three times at Universal Orlando's "Halloween Horror Nights," and now hosts his own television series, *Hacking the System* on the National Geographic channel.

Teller (of Penn and-) says, "Brian Brushwood just kills me. He's funny, dangerous, and brilliantly original. He's going to be really famous, very soon."

WATCH BRIAN'S DEMO REEL!

bit.ly/1GKK1rJ

In 2004, Brian began his first touring stage lecture, "Scams, Sasquatch, and the Supernatural: an Amazing Exposure of Pseudoscience." College audiences nationwide learn the tricks and techniques used by fake psychics, astrologers, and people who claim to speak with the dead.

WATCH THE FULL LECTURE

bit.ly/1HUy46S

Later, Brian started giving his talk "Social Engineering: Scam Your Way into Anything," an exploration of the psychology of scammers and con artists. In the talk, Brian teaches his audience how to use simple psychological tricks to achieve anything from talking their way out of a ticket to sneaking backstage at concerts . . . and, most importantly, how to recognize when someone's trying to manipulate them.

WATCH THE SOCIAL ENGINEERING LECTURE

bit.ly/1GIZtav

In 2008, Brian began hosting Scam School, the "only show dedicated to social engineering at the bar and on the street." Viewers learn quick 5-minute tips and tricks to score free drinks or to scam their friends. Scam School now boasts over one million subscribers, 400 episodes, and hundreds of millions of views.

 WATCH SCAM SCHOOL

bit.ly/1GIZyea

In addition to this book, Brian has also authored *The Professional's Guide to Fire Eating*, *Pack the House*, and *Scam School*. Visit shwood.com for information about his books, tour schedule, or to book an event.

Want to dive in to Brian's other projects?

Visit www.shwood.com for comedy albums, TV shows, and more!

 **CHECK OUT MORE OF BRIAN'S PROJECTS!**

http://bit.ly/1FFaPz1

THE BEST LETTER I'VE EVER RECEIVED

On March 2nd, 2010 (almost two years after Scam School's premiere), I received the following letter. It came from a longtime fan of both Scam School and "Night Attack" who I had not heard from in almost a year . . . and now I understand why.

Please note: the following story is so outrageous, I was convinced it had to be fake, but after several exchanges with the first-hand party, I slowly realized that the following story appears to be 100% absolutely true:

Brian,
   I am a Peace Corps volunteer, and recently did a year 'deployment' to the Dominican Republic. The village where I lived was, by all classical definitions of the word, remote. No electricity, no plumbing, and all the water comes from a hand-crank well. They grow their own crops and, literally, hunt their own dinner on a daily basis. Houses here are made by hand from mud brick and straw. The nearest established 'modern' city, La Vega, is 4 hours away by auto.
   After my year, I had grown quite close with many of the people of this community. It was one of the best experiences of my life.

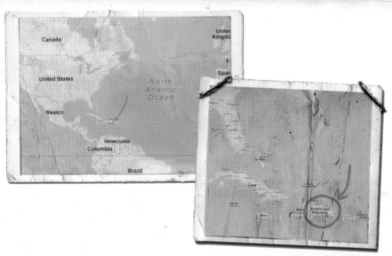

The community had a big gala celebration in
my honor on my final night before leaving to
come back to the States. During the course of
the evening, I did an impromptu magic show,
made up mostly of things I learned watching
Scam School, tweaking and changed to better
fit my audience. Well, that was the plan,
anyhow.

About 6 tricks in, I still hadn't gotten
much of a response. I'd gotten a few smatter-
ings of courtesy chuckles, but not much more
than crickets. Literally, crickets. I was
pretty sure I was not making any kind of cultural faux pas, so I took a moment and asked
one of the elders why nobody seemed that
interested or really entertained by what I
was doing. His response?

In broken English he said, "Your tricks
are very good, but we have seen them many
times before on the internet. Most of us go
to La Vega every few months. We always go to
the library and use the computers. One of the
children found a great American show called

Scam School. Maybe you watch it too when you get back to your home and one day be much better magician."

Really. God's honest truth, that happened.

As an interesting side note, you might also be interested in knowing that many of the parents in the village tease their children into behaving and going to bed on time with mocking threats of being visited by "El Diablo de Mano" (The hand devil) . . . AKA Mr. Happypants.

EXPERIENCE MR. HAPPYPANTS

bit.ly/1ERGxqt

Yes, Brian, you are known and influencing culture in remote places where even Survivorman wouldn't go. Good job! I had to write and let you know.

Congratulations, by the way, on NSFW and all the HUGE advancements you've made while I was gone. I'm looking forward to getting back into my usual routine and catching the BBliveshow. We'll always have Chadsgap. ;-)

Sincerely,

C. Thomas Kennybrook

AKA The guy that shopped the "toddler beating on a drum" picture

No surprise here: my first response was to completely disbelieve everything... but I slowly began to accept the truth when I received the follow-up email:

Good sir Brian,
That story is 110% true, although I may have mangled the exact literal quote of the village elder. I mean, there I was, in a place where they could have easily filmed Gilligan's Island, and I've got some local village elder basically telling me, "Don't quit your day job, kid. You're no Brushwood."
Totally surreal.
The funny thing about El Diablo de Mano is that I had heard it more than a handful of times while I was there, and never paid any real attention to it. Every place on Earth has their own little specific cultural nuances, and I had just kinda accepted El Diablo de Mano as one of theirs without any real thought. Once the Scam School bomb got dropped that last night, it fell into place in my head not unlike a flashback montage from some Hollywood thriller with a big reveal like The Sixth Sense or Unbreakable.

Actually, the village does have *some* electricity via four diesel generators, supplied by the Peace Corps. And they have two televisions and two iPods (also supplied by the PC). One is in the school, and the other is in a communal "movie tent" of sorts. Every few weeks on an R&R trip into La Vega, one of the PC volunteers (there were three of us) will take the iPods to the library in La Vega and load them with educational videos (for the school) and entertainment (for the movie tent). Apparently, I learned, one of the volunteers who had rotated in and back out before me used to load the entertainment iPod with Scam School. Silly me, I always picked old black and white movies. The PC has a program for educating people from the community and getting them college scholarships in the US. It's your basic investment strategy to help the community help itself. As part of lessening the culture shock, we show entertainment that not only entertains, but also is relevant with contemporary American culture. So, that's how Scam School (and Totally Rad Show) found their way into the wilds of the Dominican Republic.

I honestly don't know what to say about this, except this is a million times better than whatever my childhood dreams were.

—Brian

Part I:
DANGEROUS to MAKE YOU A STUNTS BADASS

Outrageous stunts and playing with fire... These are the highly visual openers that will turn heads and grab their attention.

COFFEE CREAMER flamethrower

IMPRESSIVENESS: 4/5

★ ★ ★ ★ ☆

CLASS: DANGEROUS STUNT

FACTORS: IMPRESSIVE FLAMES, OBVIOUSLY DANGEROUS

REQUIRES: POWDERED NON-DAIRY CREAMER

EPISODE

bit.ly/1KH58PL

AUDIO COMMENTARY

bit.ly/1F7j98W

I love this. You know those little packets of cheap, non-dairy creamer that you find at gas stations and hotel rooms? You're about to use one of those as a flamethrower.

Read that again: you're going to use non-dairy creamer . . . as a flamethrower.

Obvious Warning: **Fire is hot. And dangerous. If you try this, there's every possibility that you'll burn your face off and set the bar on fire. Also, you'll probably burn down the planet and hurt my feelings, so by all means please take proper safety precautions.**

How it Looks: In your left hand, hold a lit candle or burning lighter about waist-high. With your right hand, pour out the creamer in a fine, consistent stream, aiming the powdered cloud toward the flame (I find that it helps to use your ring finger to quickly flick at the packet as you pour). As soon as this dust cloud hits the fire, it will burst into a very large, very impressive column of fire!

VIDEO DEMO

bit.ly/1bl7rw7

Of course the fire is hot, and you may lose some arm hairs . . .
But OMG does it look awesome.

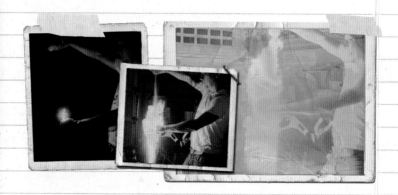

The best part is that you can't set fire to the creamer except
when it's in this cloud of dust.

VIDEO DEMO

bit.ly/1JmzfKM

Why it Works: It turns out that non-dairy creamers share many
attributes with Lycopodium powder, and as Wikipedia points out:

> Lycopodium powder is a yellow-tan dust-
> like powder historically used as a flash
> powder. It is composed of the dry spores
> of clubmoss plants, various fern relatives
> principally in the genera Lycopodium and

Diphasiastrum. When mixed with air, the spores are highly flammable because of their high fat content and their large surface area per unit of volume — a single spore's diameter is about 33 micrometers (μm).

Likewise, non-dairy creamers use vegetable fats to create that creamy texture when used in coffee, making them a good stand-in for Lycopodium powder.

Remember that you're going to make a bit of a mess wherever you try this, as unburned creamer powder will just collect on the ground. If you're worried about singeing your left hand (the fireball is definitely hot), try using a long-necked lighter.

Big thanks to Michael Ammar for teaching this one to me, and to Larry Denburg of Delaware for teaching him.

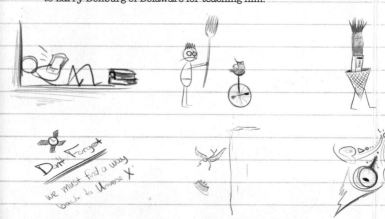

The JACK-O-LANTERN

IMPRESSIVENESS: 4/5

★ ★ ★ ★ ☆

CLASS: DANGEROUS STUNT

FACTORS: BURNS, LIGHTING CONDITIONS

REQUIRES: MATCHES

EPISODE

bit.ly/1Qfg3TM

AUDIO COMMENTARY

bit.ly/1IxFPhA

Remember the Human Chimney from Scam School Book 1? That's pretty much my all-time favorite Scam School trick. This one? A very, very close second place. The Jack-O-Lantern is the perfect follow-up to the perfect opener. It's bright, visual, surprising . . . and it looks fantastic in a darkened bar.

Oh: it's also dangerous, stupid, and will almost certainly burn you sooner or later. But oh, man does it look good.

The Effect: Placing a lit match inside your mouth, you do a very convincing impression of a grinning jack-o-lantern . . . all without burning yourself.

The Warning: Before attempting this trick, ask yourself: Are you prepared to actually burn yourself while learning this?

Do you have what it takes? Because you will burn yourself while learning how to do this right.

It's okay if the answer's "No." You can just go learn a card trick instead. Or maybe a math puzzle. Or maybe you can memorize a funny limerick... Everybody loves puns, right? Sure! I'm certain that limericks and puns will be every bit as big a hit as being the guy who puts fire inside his mouth and smiles.

VIDEO DEMO

bit.ly/1D5Tyr5

The Work: We're going to start small and build up to something impressive. Start by sitting in front of a mirror with a bowl of ice cubes and some matches. Suck on the ice cubes for a bit to cool the roof of your mouth, then strike a match. You're going to put the match into your mouth flaming-end first and bite down on the base, while making sure to inhale slowly the entire time. This action of inhaling will draw the heat down into your lungs and keep it off the roof of your mouth, while the flame illuminates your mouth from the inside.

Keep in mind that even this small amount of fire is still very, very hot … all hydrocarbons burn at temperatures up to 2000 degrees Fahrenheit. If you don't inhale slowly, you'll cook the roof of your mouth.

To get the mechanics down, practice with an unlit match. Get to where you can confidently and quickly place the match right into position. The more you hesitate doing the Jack-O-Lantern, the bigger chance you'll have of burning yourself. Only try it with a lit match once you're confident in the moves.

When you do start working with a lit match, the odds are good that you'll inhale too quickly, blowing out the match. Keep trying in front of the mirror, inhaling less and less each time until you get a decent glow. Practice will allow you to strike a balance between the brightness in your mouth and the heat of the flame.

The good news about burns inside the mouth is that they heal very quickly, due to the phenomenal amount of blood that pumps through the mouth, lips, and tongue. A couple of days should set you right to try again.

Note: When (not if) you burn your mouth, it will almost always be a first-degree burn. Refer to this page from the Mayo Clinic for simple care to treat minor burns.

mayocl.in/1aYY2X2

the HUMAN BLOCKHEAD

IMPRESSIVENESS: 5/5

★ ★ ★ ★ ★

CLASS: DANGEROUS STUNT

FACTORS: DANGEROUS, HIGHLY UNCOMFORTABLE

REQUIRES: GRIT, Q-TIPS, NAILS

EPISODE

bit.ly/1cdtSni

AUDIO COMMENTARY

bit.ly/1QagnUD

You asked, you pleaded.

I hinted, I teased.

And at long last, I FINALLY revealed how the Human Blockhead stunt works on Scam School. Not sure it was the smartest thing I've ever done, but it's really nothing more than simple biology. Really gross biology.

Q-TIP DEMO

bit.ly/1P5yoC3

First off, let me be clear: shoving anything up your nose is a bad idea. Nobody should do it except under the supervision of an expert. All of this is for your informational edification only.

Essentially, you've got two major sets of sinuses in your head: your frontals (above your eyes), and your maxillary sinuses (the big ones that curve down to become your throat). It's possible to push a skinny object (like a nail) into either of them, but the frontal sinuses are a REALLY BAD idea, since there's mere millimeters of soft tissue separating the nail from YOUR FREAKING BRAIN.

The blockhead's properly performed by inserting the nail into the maxillary sinus, straight back until it touches the back of your throat. Check out this clip from CNN for more proper, "scientific" detail.

CHECK OUT BRIAN EXPLAINING
THE HUMAN BLOCKHEAD ON CNN

bit.ly/1JbQSxd

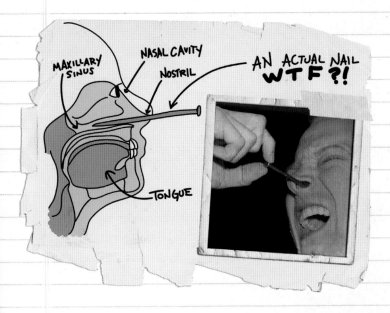

MAXILLARY SINUS

NASAL CAVITY

NOSTRIL

AN ACTUAL NAIL **WTF?!**

TONGUE

If you want to learn the blockhead, start with a q-tip: wet it with your mouth, then slide it around in your nostril for a bit. Get comfortable; make yourself at home. Get to know every nook and cranny (yes, this is gross, but so is the human blockhead effect!).

Fun fact: if you're in a coma, this is how they shove a feeding tube down to your stomach!

NAIL DEMO

bit.ly/1QagsHU

If you aim the q-tip straight back towards your throat, you should be able to drag it across the bottominsides of your sinus cavity until it hits a flap leading back into the deeper sinus. Once you're past that flap, it will keep going straight back until it hits your throat. (Be smart here: don't push the q-tip so far back that you lose your grip on it. That would be an embarrassing trip to the emergency room.)

From here on out, it's just a matter of testing your own limits and practicing. Over time, you'll toughen up your soft tissues as you switch to thin nails, then thicker nails, then spoons, then the forearms of babies, subway trains . . . I suppose the sky's the limit.

In all seriousness: don't be stupid about this one. If you're careless, you'll give yourself a giant nosebleed and feel like a total idiot. I also don't recommend getting into a bar fight with a nail in your nose, as one punch to the face will send the nail into your brain stem.

For those wondering how practical this effect is at the bar: I do it all the time, using drink-mixers and cocktail straws. They don't feel all that great, but the effect definitely shocks and impresses. Best of all, the impromptu nature convinces people that there's no trick to the Human Blockhead.

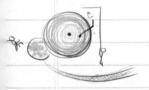

CUT a LIME in HALF with a CIGARETTE!

AUDIO COMMENTARY

bit.ly/1bdGgCO

EPISODE

bit.ly/1zsQLgI

IMPRESSIVENESS: 5/5
★ ★ ★ ★ ★

CLASS: DANGEROUS STUNT

FACTORS: ELABORATE SETUP, AMAZING PAYOFF
REQUIRES: LIME, CIGARETTE, MATCHES, ICE CUBES

It's a pretty rare treat when I run across a bar trick that's like nothing I've ever seen before. This one has an unbelievable setup and an even more unbelievable payoff. It came to me from comedian Chuck

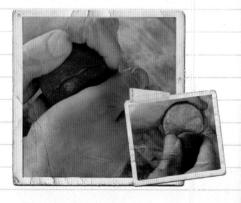

Savage, who said he heard it came from the
Texas state prison system.

The Setup: Grab a cigarette. Grab a
lime. (Both should be in ample supply at the
bar)

The Challenge: Use the cigarette to
cut the lime in half. No fingernails and no
other tools can touch the lime.

The Secret: Soak your fingers in some cold ice water (you'll
understand why in a bit). Put the cigarette in your mouth
BACKWARDS and light the filter. While the filter burns, pinch the
melting fiberglass (or whatever it is) into the sharp shape of a
scalpel. This will put out the flame, and, once cooled, will create a
very hard, sharp cutting surface for your lime! I've actually since
been told that this knife-making trick is the reason that prisoners
on suicide watch aren't allowed to have cigarettes.

Once you've made your "knife," simply cut through the rind
along the equator of your lime. Once you make the cut all around, it
will easily tear in half!

VIDEO DEMO

bit.ly/1bdGeuB

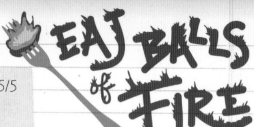

EAT BALLS of FIRE

IMPRESSIVENESS: 5/5

★ ★ ★ ★ ★

CLASS: OPENER/STUNT

FACTORS: FACTORS: FIRE (OBVIOUSLY)

REQUIRES: 100% PURE COTTON BALLS, FLAME

EPISODE

bit.ly/1AAOvRs

AUDIO COMMENTARY

bit.ly/1DDVxXi

This is awesome. Just by keeping some cotton balls in your pocket, you'll be set to completely shock everyone next time you're at a party or bar.

How it Looks: You walk up to burning tiki torch or bar candle, examine it intently, and then reach in and tear out a piece of flaming ember. Without pause, you toss the fiery coal into your mouth and chew it up... all while remaining completely unharmed.

VIDEO DEMO

bit.ly/1IxG1gK

How it's Done: This one's half stunt, half-magic trick.

The effect is pretty clean looking: it really does look like you're tearing off a chunk of the torch and swallowing burning embers. In actuality, you'll be eating a fiery cotton ball.

To practice, grab some cotton balls (make sure they're made of 100% cotton, as any synthetic fibers will literally melt in your mouth) and stick them in your back pocket. Approach a burning tiki torch, reach into your pocket and "palm" the cotton (see illustrations).

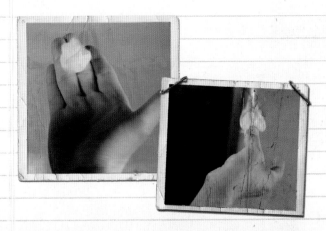

There's really nothing difficult about this; you're just holding the cotton, pinched between your middle and ring fingers while allowing your hand to dangle loosely by your side.

VIDEO DEMO WITH TORCH

bit.ly/1EkeZfO

Give an intent look at the torch and bring your hand up to the wick with the cotton facing toward you, pinch the cotton toward the wick, and then pivot your hand as you pull away, revealing the cotton as you do. This motion should appear like a plucking or ripping motion to the audience. In performance, the cotton will ignite, and it will seem like you've torn out a bit of the flame to toss in your mouth.

Now here's the tricky part: as soon as you ignite the cotton ball, stick out your tongue. Place the burning cotton on the center

VIDEO DEMO WITH CANDLE

bit.ly/1P5yxFQ

of your tongue, use your fingers and tongue to push it all the way inside your mouth, and simply close your lips.

Since the cotton ball ignites quickly and burns slowly, closing your mouth will instantly snuff out the flame long before the cotton gets hot enough to do any damage. In fact, the most common mistake people make with this effect is taking too long to put the cotton in their mouths. The longer you hold the cotton, the sooner it will burn your fingertips. Just light it and place it into your mouth.

Some people think it'll look cooler to simply toss the cotton into their open mouth, but that's probably a bad idea. It's surprisingly hard to aim flaming cotton at your own mouth, and you don't want to miss your target and bounce the fireball onto the floor.

If you don't think you can convincingly pull off the magic moves to "pluck" out the cotton, you can perform this effect simply as a stunt: just pull out a cotton ball, light it, and toss it in your mouth. That's still something they don't see everyday!

Note: You're playing with fire here. Remember you'll only have a couple of seconds of holding the cotton ball before it will begin to burn your finger-tips . . . make sure you take sensible precautions when doing this or ANY other fire related acts! Make sure you have a fire extinguisher nearby and (most importantly), a plan for how to deal with any mishaps.

IMPRESSIVENESS: 3/5

★ ★ ★ ☆ ☆

CLASS: OPENER

FACTORS: DANGER, BURNS

REQUIRES: CIGARETTE, DISREGARD FOR SAFETY

EPISODE

bit.ly/1OU9EjE

AUDIO COMMENTARY

bit.ly/1DDVE5b

These are a pretty badass couple of stunts. If you do them right, you won't burn yourself, but you will have a god-awful taste in your mouth. Oh, and you'll also impress the hell out of your friends.

Putting out a Cigarette on Your Tongue

The Effect: Look your friend dead in the eye, and with a straight face, announce that you're going to put a cigarette out on your tongue. . . . and then you do it!

There's no sleight of hand, no switches, no copping out: you actually put a cigarette out on your tongue.

The Work: To minimize the chances of getting burned, you're going to lightly and quickly dab the cigarette on your tongue in different places each time. The moisture on your tongue snuffs out the fire, and repeatedly moving to another place ensures no one spot on your tongue gets too warm.

When you try this the first time, use an ice cube to chill down your tongue (this really will make a difference). Also, make sure to ash your cigarette so there's as little hanging ash as possible . . . the less hanging ash there is, the faster the cigarette will extinguish.

Next, stick out your tongue as wide and as flat as you can, leaving as much saliva on your tongue as you're able. Finally: tap,

tap, tap the burning cigarette in a pattern around your tongue. Your goal is to spread the heat around as much as you can, while your saliva extinguishes the embers.

After 10–15 taps, the cigarette should be totally out, and your tongue will be totally black. You can add an extra flourish by grinding the (now fully extinguished) cigarette into your tongue. This extra flourish will cause them to remember the effect as you simply grinding it out on your tongue.

The taste will be awful, but whatever you do, don't react to it. I mean, you've come this far looking awesome . . . don't ruin the effect over some nasty ash taste.

The Match on Tongue

This one's much simpler. Strike a wooden or cardboard match, stick out your tongue wide and flat (just like you did with the cigarette), and wipe the match down your tongue. You'll hear a satisfying sizzle, and the match will go completely out.

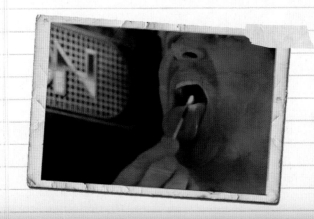

Remember that the longer the match burns, the more weakened the match will become. If you take too long building up the nerve, when you wipe the match on your tongue there's a chance that the head will break off. Once that happens, the heat of the burned match head will sit in one place, giving you a nasty burn on your tongue.

VIDEO DEMO

bit.ly/1yLfbSu

Part II: SIMPLE CHEATS with HUGE PAYOFFS

NEVER PLAY FAIR! Whether it's running a rigged game or playing a friendly round of chess... these scams will give YOU the house edge.

The GOVERNMENT Conspiracy

AUDIO COMMENTARY

bit.ly/1086clc

EPISODE

bit.ly/1EOvcRd

IMPRESSIVENESS: 3/5

★ ★ ★ ☆ ☆

CLASS: TWEENER

FACTOR'S: EXTREMELY VERSATILE

REQUIRES: REMOTE PARTNER

This one's a classic that just about all magicians know, and it's unbelievably powerful: It uses no spies, no technology, can be done from anywhere, and the method is diabolically simple.

Picture This: You're at a bar, tucked away in a corner with your friend. You make sure nobody's watching. You have him check your body for secret spy cams or recording devices. Once he's satisfied that nobody could possibly know what the two of you are up to, have him shuffle a deck of playing cards.

"Mix them up really well," you remind him. Only after he's completely convinced that there's no possible way for you to know the order of the cards, have him cut the deck and flip over a card.

"Hmm . . . the three of spades, huh? You want to stick to that one, or change your mind? Hell, if you want, you can even pick your favorite card from your own mind."

Feeling suspicious, he replaces the three of spades, instead drawing the seven of hearts. Tapping it twice, he verifies his final choice.

"Okay, quick: turn that card back over so nobody can see it. I'll tell you for a fact, that there's no possible way I could have known that you'd pick that card. But you know who did know?" you ask as you glance around the room.

"The Government."

"Here, I'll prove it to you. I'll call them right now," you say as you pull out your cell phone and make a call. After a couple of rings, your friend listens to you ask "Hello? . . .Yes, can I please speak to The Government?"

Then after a short pause, you hand over the phone, and your friend hears:

"Hello. This is The Government. We've seen everything, and we know you chose the seven of hearts."

The Method: In this case, we called the third party "The Government," though you could easily call him "the wizard" or even "the devil."

Just arrange with a friend to play the part of "The Government," and work out a simple code with him before hand: when you call, your friend will answer not with "yes?" or "hello?" but simply by slowly calling out the suits of a deck of cards: "clubs . . . hearts . . . spades . . . diamonds . . ." The moment you hear the correct suit of the selected card, say "Yes, hello?" and that will indicate the correct suit to your accomplice.

Next, he'll start calling out card values. Listen to him say "ace . . . two . . . three . . ." and as soon as you hear the value of the chosen card, say "Hi, may I speak to The Government?" and hand over the phone.

It's unbustable! If they're suspicious of your phone, volunteer to use their phone. Or better yet, volunteer to call The Government from a payphone . . . In a world surrounded by high-tech listening and watching devices, this low-tech code is a masterwork.

BE A (FAKE!) LIE DETECTOR

AUDIO COMMENTARY

bit.ly/1DtHmRq

EPISODE

bit.ly/1AA18dI

IMPRESSIVENESS: 4/5

★ ★ ★ ★ ☆

CLASS: TWEENER

FACTORS: VALUABLE UTILITY METHOD

REQUIRES: A SHINER (READ ON TO FIND OUT MORE!)

You're about to prove that you're an expert lie detector. You'll always be able to tell when they're lying and when they're telling the truth. You will never, ever be wrong, and they'll be certain you've got a supreme gift for reading faces!

Except for one tiny, minor detail: you're a complete fraud.

The Setup: The setup couldn't be simpler. A borrowed deck of cards is totally shuffled and a random card is selected. There are no marked cards, no forces, and the sucker truly does have a free choice of their card.

Once they pull their card from the deck, you'll begin asking a series of questions about their card. They can choose to lie or tell

the truth as you ask them "Is it a red card?" "Is it an even number?" "Is your card a spade?"

Whether they choose to lie or tell the truth for each response, their job is to look as honest as possible. Your job is to watch their faces for clues, and bust them when they lie.

Amazingly, it doesn't matter what they say, as you're ALWAYS able to tell when they're lying!

The Scam: Everything here is window dressing. You don't have to know the first thing about spotting a liar; you just need to know their card, which is why you use a "shiner."

A shiner is any shiny object that can be used to catch the reflection of a card . . . it could be a cup of black coffee, a silver lighter, or (in this case) your cell phone. By leaving your cell phone on the table, when you spread the cards out in front of your sucker, you'll be able to see the reflections from underneath . . . allowing you to know their card before even THEY do.

VIDEO DEMO

bit.ly/1E2aKDO

Cell phones are the perfect shiner, as they're socially invisible. We see them so often that as long as one's turned off, we completely fail to notice them. In addition to cell phones, if you look you'll notice natural shiners around you. It could be a shiny button on the upholstery, a decorative mirror, or even a cup of black coffee. Once you find a wellplaced shiner, you're set to blow their minds.

When you're performing any kind of lie-detector routine, remember that the key is convincing them that you really are reading their facial expressions. Each time I ask a question, I'll repeat it 3 times. While they answer, I'll carefully watch their eyes, eyebrows, posture, and head position. If they blink 2 of the 3 times, I'll point that out: "Aha! You blinked both times, which is a lying cue . . . that was a lie, wasn't it?" If they nod or shake their head, I'll point that out as my evidence. Even a nonsense cue can be used: "I noticed that you leaned slightly back, which would indicate confidence . . . that tells me you're telling the truth and that it IS a spade . . . Am I right?"

Just remember that the key to this presentation is believability. If they really think you're a genius of body posture and facial expressions, that's WAY more impressive than just being able to guess their card.

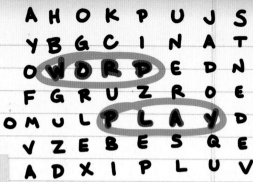

```
A H O K P U J S
Y B G C I N A T
O W O R D E D N
F G R U Z R O E
O M U L P L A Y D
V Z E B E S Q E
A D X I P L U V
```

IMPRESSIVENESS: 3/5

★ ★ ★ ☆ ☆

CLASS: OPENER

FACTORS: AUDIENCE INVOLVEMENT

REQUIRES: NOTHING

EPISODE

bit.ly/1K8bKFK

AUDIO COMMENTARY

bit.ly/1D7pzjK

Think you are good with words? What if I took a bunch of letters and ripped them away from the alphabet... How many words could you still spell? Let's find out, and score a free beer while we do it.

The Setup: Grab any two people at the bar and find out which of the two is the better wordsmith. Start with Mr. Wordsmith and give him 90 seconds to think up as many words as he possibly can without using the letters A, B, C, or J, K, M, or P. Keep a running tally of how many he gets.

The Bet: After the wordsmith takes his turn, offer a twist: not only will you bet that Ms. Not-so-good-with-words will come up with more words in less time, but that she'll be able to come up with over 50 words in less than 90 seconds. You'll help her only by contributing five words to her list.

The Twist: Once Mr. Wordsmith says "go," look Ms. not-good-withwords in the eyes and carefully start listing your first five words: "One," "Two," "Three," "Four," and "Five." She'll immediately figure out where this is headed, and continue to count off numbers all the way up to fifty, winning the game!

The key to this scam is in the non-verbal communication: before you contribute your words, make sure you have her full attention and make sure she understands that there's a specific reason for the words you're choosing. If she doesn't pick up on the fact that all your numbers fit the rules, then you're stuck.

Magicians call this creating an "instant stooge," and picking the right kind of person for this technique is extremely important. Little gestures like leaning in, deliberate eye contact, or an arm on her shoulder will help to clue her in that something important is about to happen.

WIN $ CASH AT DARTS

AUDIO COMMENTARY

bit.ly/1yK6rf6

EPISODE

bit.ly/1ELtWnv

IMPRESSIVENESS: 3/5

★★★☆☆

CLASS: BAR BET

FACTOR'S: ODDS-BASED BET

REQUIRES: $20 AND A DART BOARD

Suck at darts? You can still make BANK with this simple scam, and you don't even need to take a shot!

Here's the scam: Pin a $20 to the dartboard and offer it to

whomever can hit it 3 times in a row, following your simple rules:

1. The first toss must be from the line.
2. The second toss must be from one step in front of the line.
3. The third toss must be from one step behind the line.

Charge a buck a turn. Watch the Washingtons roll in as

your trusting dupes fail over and over at this deceptively hard

challenge. Eventually, odds are that someone will win the twenty,

but you'll be well in the black by then.

There's two important part of this scam that make it a

moneymaker for you:

1. Compound probability: Let's say someone's pretty good at

darts, and has a 75% chance of hitting the $20 each time. That may sound pretty good, but that means the odds of him hitting the $20 three times in a row are only 42%!

2. Altering the landscape: The fact that each throw is from a different distance is highly disorienting. Worse yet is the fact that the most difficult of the three throws is last.

Remember that it's not impossible for you to lose on this scam. In our trials it took 40-60 tries before someone finally hit it 3 times in a row . . . but if someone lucks out and nails it on the first try, be gracious and just move on to the next trick. That's why you're learning hundreds of these: you'll make it up over the rest of the night!

AN EASY MAGIC SQUARE CHEAT

IMPRESSIVENESS: 3/5

★ ★ ★ ☆ ☆

CLASS: TWEENER

FACTORS: FAKE INTELLIGENCE, SOMEWHAT TEDIOUS EFFECT

REQUIRES: PAPER AND PEN

AUDIO COMMENTARY

bit.ly/1aL6XOD

EPISODE

bit.ly/1FlIanH

This one comes from the genius mind of my friend MIT Rob.

He's easily one of my favorite magical thinkers, and he came up

with a way to fake having crazy-smart, Rain-Man-like math skills

So here's the thing: mathemagicians have the super-smart ability to take any random number and create a "magic square" based on it. A magic square looks like it's just filled with random numbers, but the twist is that all the numbers in every row, column, diagonal, and quadrant will add up to the volunteer's selected number.

It's super-impressive and also super-hard to do. You gotta be smart with math and stuff. I'd rather look like a mad genius anytime by faking a magic square.

The Work: You're going to start by "freely selecting" a "totally random" number, using the following steps:

Write out the digits 1-16 in a 4x4 square. Ask someone to circle any digit they want and then cross out all the remaining digits in the same row and column.

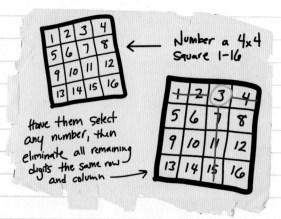

Then, have them pass the square over and ask the next person to do the same thing (using any remaining digits). Continue until four numbers are selected and add them up to determine a "secret number" to be used for the experiment.

Here's the twist: no matter which numbers are selected, the result will always be 34. This is critical, because the magic square you "spontaneously" figure out is actually a pre-determined configuration that works ONLY for the number 34!

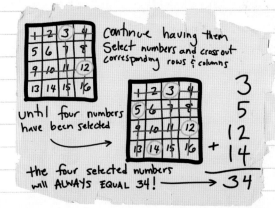

Once you've selected a number, draw in a deep breath, close your eyes, and act like you're pulling some major mental gymnastics. Then snap into action like a mad genius and quickly start filling in an empty 4x4 square just like so:

16 - 3 - 2 - 13

5 - 10 - 11 - 8

9 - 6 - 7 - 12

4 - 15 - 14 - 1

Here's an easy pattern to remember when creating this result.

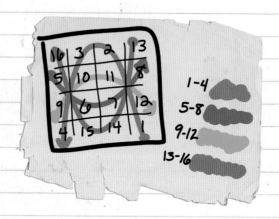

Finally, show your friends that what you've created "on-the-fly" is actually a magic square . . . all 4 rows add up to 34. All 4 columns add up to 34. The four numbers in the middle add up to 34. The four corners add up to 34 . . . even all 4 numbers in each quadrant add up to 34.

You're a damned wizard!

VIDEO DEMO

bit.ly/1DtIZ1t

Just remember to look like what you're doing is really, really hard, and definitely take full credit for being a genius when you're done.

Psychic Dice

IMPRESSIVENESS: 3/5

★ ★ ★ ☆ ☆

CLASS: TWEENER

FACTORS: CASUAL MINDREADING, BEST WHEN PLAYED LOW-KEY

REQUIRES: 3 DICE, CLEAR GLASS

AUDIO COMMENTARY

bit.ly/1H8pDpO

EPISODE

bit.ly/1IG9ozJ

This one's not exactly rocket science, but it's a simple trick that'll occupy your friends while you prove to them you've got psychic powers:

The Setup: Three dice are dropped into a glass, covered with a coaster, then shaken up. The mark makes absolutely sure that nobody else can peek as he lifts the glass up over his head and looks up through the bottom of the glass. He adds up the values of the bottom sides of all three dice, memorizes his secret number, and carefully replaces the glass on the table.

Without peeking or cheating, the scam artist is able to divine the secret number in the sucker's mind!

The Work: The method is simple, but the trick is pulling it off with subtlety. Amazingly, most people do not know that dice are made such that the values on opposite sides always total 7. (If there's a 6 on one side, there will be a 1 on the other. If one side has a value of 3, the opposite side will have a value of 4, etc.) So by catching a quick glimpse of the tops of the dice, you can figure out the values on the bottom.

You could look at each individual die and figure out what value is on the other side, or use a simple shortcut to get the total value on bottom: total up the values on the top of the dice, and subtract that amount from 21. The result will be the secret number they're thinking of!

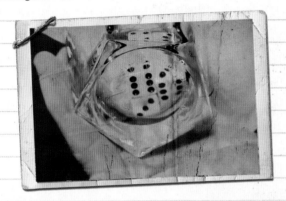

Now remember that they're going to suspect you're somehow peeking . . . so don't go for the gold right away. Instead, when they set down the glass, maintain eye contact, and act like you've already got the answer. After a moment, make a distracting gesture and sneak just a peek at the top of the dice, and you'll be home free.

Or better yet, catch a glimpse as soon as they've finished shaking up the dice. Immediately after you've peeked, turn your head away and insist that you don't want to be accused of seeing the dice when he lifts the glass. While your head is turned, do your math, and you'll know their total before they do!

 M4RE Pool Hall SCAMS

IMPRESSIVENESS: 3/5–4/5

★ ★ ★ ☆ ☆

CLASS: NASTY PRANKS, CLOSERS

FACTORS: VARIABLE RELIABILITY, IMPRESSIVENESS

REQUIRES: POOL TABLE, CIGARETTE OR GOLF TEE

EPISODE ONE

bit.ly/1IG9CHa

EPISODE TWO

bit.ly/1GVzH5R

Wow, there are a LOT of pool hall scams out there. We covered a few of them in the first Scam School book, but it's never like you can know too many ways to score a buck at the pool table, right?

#1: The Best/Worst Pool Trick Shot

This one's awesome because the challenge is to not pull off an impressive trick shot.

The Setup: Place a cigarette, golf tee, nail, or bolt upright on the circle sticker in the center of a pool table. Next, set up three balls surrounding it (two in front, one in back), making sure that the bolt is touching one of the two balls in front.

Now, get everyone's attention and promise to blow them away. Slam the cue ball into the triangle of balls, knocking down the bolt. As soon as this happens, jump up and down and act like you just juggled eight chainsaws (though your friends will be less than impressed).

Offer to show them again: Do everything the same way, and knock over the bolt a second time.

The Twist: Tell them it's much, much harder than it looks. In fact, bet them a beer that they WON'T be able to knock over the bolt when they try. Once they accept, set up the balls and bolt almost the same way you did the first time, only this time, make sure the bolt is touching the single ball in back.

Thanks to Newtonian physics, when they slam the balls, the bolt will remain standing and you'll win a free drink!

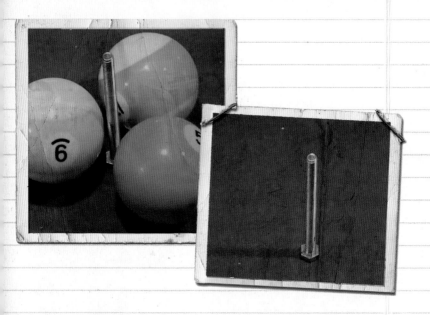

Remember, it's important that the object in the middle have a very thin shaft and wide base (golf tees are perfect). If you're using a cigarette, there's a good chance it will fall over, so you just may want to demonstrate this as a straight-up trick shot. In that case, just set up the cigarette (touching the back ball), and fire your cueball at one of the two front balls. The cigarette will still be standing, and you'll at least look like a badass.

#2: Under the Cue

The Setup: Set a cue stick across a pool table, and challenge your friend to "roll any ball from one side of the table to the other, without hitting the cue stick"

The Payoff: After all your friends failed attempts, show him

how easy it is by simply rolling the ball forward . . . under the table.

#3: The Ball-buster

A while back, a fan sent me this video of the ultimate nasty pool-

hall trick shot prank. The trick was so good, so perfect, that I refused

to believe it worked in real life. I insisted we test it out on the show.

Much to my surprise, not only does it work . . . but it works

shockingly well.

The Challenge: Your friend stands at the opposite end of the pool table from you, keeping one finger on the top of each ball positioned right in front of the two corner pockets. Place a quarter or fifty-cent piece right on the spot sticker, and you're ready to go.

"Ready?" you ask, "Here it comes: I'll bet you a beer that even with your hands on those two balls, I'll be able to hit both balls in just one shot."

It sounds crazy. With his fingers on both of them, there's no chance you can ricochet off of one ball and hit the other. Of course he accepts the challenge, and you get ready for your shot.

The Twist: Imagine his surprise when, with full force, you slam the cue ball straight towards the quarter. The cue ball strikes the quarter, hops up into the air . . .

. . . and slams right into his crotch.

Congratulations, you did it. You managed to hit both balls with just one shot. (Now buy your friend a beer and apologize.)

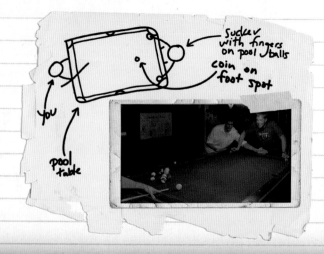

CHEAT WITH "NON-TRANSITIVE" DICE

AUDIO COMMENTARY

bit.ly/1P5AAcR

EPISODE ONE

bit.ly/1zI9tkP

This sweet little scam absolutely breaks my brain. It's 100% fair and open, and 100% skewed in your favor. You'll have to invest a little time to make these special dice, but once you have them, you'll be set for years.

The Setup: First, make yourself a set of "non-transitive dice." These are dice that are completely ungimmicked, but they have a different set of values on each side of the die than you would normally find. All you'll need is 6 dice and some model airplane paint. Paint 2 of the dice completely green, 2 completely red, and 2 completely blue.

Next, assign number values as you see here:

Red: 1 4 4 4 4 4

Green: 2 2 2 5 5 5

Blue: 3 3 3 3 3 6

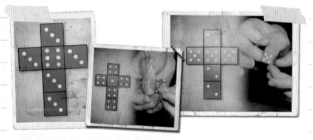

If you don't want to spend the time to make your own, Google "nontransitive dice" and you'll be able to buy some pre-made online. Just make sure they're the same style as the ones we're making here.

The Game: Set out one die of each color, and challenge your sucker to pick any dice for a head-to-head "best of ten" challenge. Feel free to let them examine the dice and freely let him consider which values are most likely to win. Once he picks his die, you pick yours accordingly:

If he picks Red, you pick Green

If he picks Green, you pick Blue

If he picks Blue, you pick Red

In a match of 10 throws, you will almost always win. It sounds crazy, but each one of these three non-transitive dice is designed to beat out one of the other two. Here are the numbers:

In a face-off between Green and Red, GREEN wins each roll roughly 58% of the time

In a face-off between Blue and Green, BLUE wins each roll roughly 58% of the time

In a face-off between Red and Blue, RED wins each roll a whopping 69% of the time!

The Twist: Here's the best part of the scam: after you've won a few times, you can completely explain how you're winning, but STILL beat the sucker! Once you've gotten a couple of free drinks, explain exactly how the dice work and which color will beat each other color. Then offer to play one more time to test their understanding . . . but this time, use two dice of each color to play.

Amazingly, when you double the number of dice, the advantages flip completely in the other direction! For example:

In a face-off with TWO dice between Green and Red, RED wins each roll roughly 59% of the time

In a face-off with TWO dice between Blue and Green, GREEN wins each roll roughly 59% of the time

In a face-off with TWO dice between Red and Blue, BLUE wins each roll roughly 52% of the time (notice the small margin of victory on this one, and remember it . . . you might want to go for best of 20 if they pick Red).

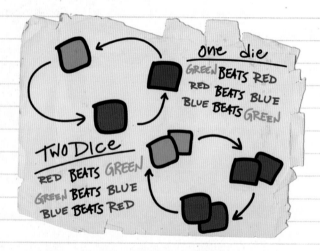

one die
GREEN BEATS RED
RED BEATS BLUE
BLUE BEATS GREEN

TWO DICE
RED BEATS GREEN
GREEN BEATS BLUE
BLUE BEATS RED

The fact that you're not 100% guaranteed to win makes this a surprisingly fun scam to pull on your friends. Trust me: the extra effort to make or buy the dice is well worth it on this game.

IMPOSSIBLE KNOT

IMPRESSIVENESS: 3/5

★ ★ ★ ☆ ☆

CLASS: FAKE (IMPOSSIBLE) SKILL

FACTORS: FRUSTRATE FRIENDS

REQUIRES: TIE OR ROPE

Sometimes you need a scam that serves absolutely no function but to make your friends miserable. Something that makes you look smart and makes them look dumb. This is one of those scams.

The Setup: Grab about 3 feet of rope (or just use your necktie) and remind your friends of what every elementary student knows: it's absolutely impossible to tie an overhand knot without letting go of the rope at least once.

You can kinda fake it by crossing your arms before you pick up the rope. When you unwind your arms apart from each other, the rope will tie itself into an overhand knot. But that's not what we're about to do. We're about to learn a secret, incredible variation of the overhand knot that (amazingly!) can be tied without ever letting go of either end of the rope . . . (I promise! There's no way this will just be a big trick to make me look smart and make you look dumb!)

The Moves: Check out the videos and photos for reference, but essentially there are 4 moves to remember, and they're pretty simple:

1. Start by holding each end of the rope and make a backwards "J" in front of your left arm.

2. Pull down the top of the "J" over your left arm. You'll now discover you've made 2 holes side-by-side.

3. Run your right arm out through the left hole, then back in through the right-hand hole.

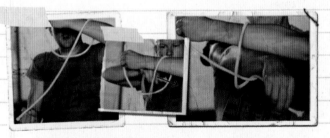

4. Finally, toss the whole mess forward off your wrists, and you'll discover a neatly-tied overhand knot. Ta-da!

Say, why are you so frustrated? Didn't it work for you? So odd . . . it works for me every time. Maybe you just need to try it one more time.

VIDEO (LIE DEMO)

bit.ly/1P5AHVV

The Secret: Part of the beauty of this scam is that almost all the moves are legitimate. There's only one extra, secret move that you leave out of your instructions:

- After step 3, you'll find you're holding a big, confusing tangle of rope. Turn your palms facing outward and you'll discover a small section near the end of the rope right in front of your right hand.

- Notice that your right-hand thumb and forefinger are busy pinching the end of the rope, but your remaining fingers are able pinch down on that little section of rope against your palm.

- Here's your secret move: At the exact moment that you toss the rope forward off your wrists, pinch that little section of rope with your right-hand fingers and let go with your thumb and forefingers. When executed at full-speed, this tiny move will be undetectable, and all anyone will see is the tumble of rope falling forward and creating an overhand knot.

Magicians call this the principle of "the big move covering the little move," and it's astonishingly effective. Just practice the moves three or four times, and you'll be shocked at how quickly you get this down.

VIDEO (SECRET DEMO)

bit.ly/1EkgcTK

There's even a fun subtlety that will convince at least one of your friends they've got it right: as you're giving instructions, walk them all the way up to part 3, then tell them to freeze: "See?" you say, "You've already got it! Here, look . . ."

Reach over to grab each tip of the rope and ask them to let go and pull their hands out from the ropes. Once the hands are gone, you'll be left holding an overhand knot. Of course, this is a blatant violation of the "don't let go" rule you just set up for them, but they'll experience it as proof that they had the moves right and that your knot isn't just a big lie.

(Which, of course, it is.)

VIDEO (TUTORIAL DEMO)

bit.ly/1aL7bVQ

LAY DOWN the (PROBABILITY) LAW

IMPRESSIVENESS: 4/5

★ ★ ★ ★ ☆

CLASS: RIGGED GAME

FACTORS: COUNTER INTUITIVE, HEADY

REQUIRES: INTERNET CONNECTIVITY

I know everything in this book is supposed to be fake and tricky. But to me, the scientific principle behind this trick is nothing short of real, actual universe-shaking magic. I don't claim to understand it; I seek only to harness its power for free beers.

The Offer: Grab a smartphone (or even faster, corner your friend in his cubicle at work) and offer to play a game. The two of you will take turns looking up the most completely random-ass numbers you can think of: The length (in feet) of the Rio Grande river. The current stock price of Apple (in US dollars). The mass of the sun (in kilograms). The number of calories in 3 gallons of mint chocolate chip ice cream.

Use Google or WolframAlpha.com to get answers, and score points by looking at the first digit of each random-ass number and using the following rules: if the first digit is a 1, 2, or 3, you get a point. If the first digit is a 5, 6, 7, 8, or 9, your sucker gets a point. If it starts with 4, nobody gets a point.

The Fix: On the surface, this sounds like you're screwed. I mean, your opponent has almost twice the number of possible ways to win, and if the numbers are truly random, then it stands to reason that he'll be right almost twice as often. How could this possibly be a smart bet for the scammer?

The Law: Because of an amazing mathematical rule called "Benford's Law." It defies all intuition and says that in just about any naturallyoccurring random number, the odds are over 60% that the first digit will be a 1, 2 or 3.

From Wikipedia:

Benford's law, also called the first-digit law, states that in lists of numbers from many (but not all) real-life sources of data, the

leading digit is distributed in a specific, nonuniform way. According to this law, the first digit is 1 about 30% of the time, and larger digits occur as the leading digit with lower and lower frequency, to the point where 9 as a first digit occurs less than 5% of the time. This distribution of first digits is the same as the widths of gridlines on the logarithmic scale. Benford's law also gives the expected distribution for digits beyond the first, which approach a uniform distribution as the digit place goes to the right.

This result has been found to apply to a wide variety of data sets, including electricity bills, street addresses, stock prices, population numbers, death rates, lengths of rivers, physical and mathematical constants, and processes described by power laws (which are very common in nature). It tends to be most accurate when values are distributed across multiple orders of magnitude.

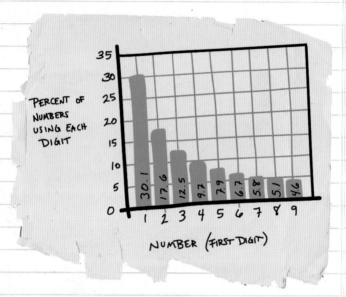

In our game, that means that for any completely random number, you have a 60% chance of getting a point, while they only have a 30% chance... Even with half the numbers, you have a 2-to-1 advantage over them!

You really ought to try this one out on yourself. Half the fun is picking insanely weird random numbers to look up.

IMPRESSIVENESS: 3/5

★ ★ ★ ☆ ☆

CLASS: TWEENER

FACTORS: PROCESS HEAVY,
REQUIRES COOPERATION

REQUIRES: BORROWED
SMARTPHONE

EPISODE

bit.ly/1ERM402

AUDIO COMMENTARY

bit.ly/1D7pT1V

Diamond Jim Tyler is incredibly talented, his Bamboozler books are excellent, and having him on Scam School was an absolute blast. This was the first trick he shared with us; not only is it a fooler, but it's a sneaky way to get the girl's phone number without her even knowing how you did it!

The Work: Start by writing down a prediction on the back of a napkin, and have any girl pull out her cell phone to do a few crazy calculations.

"I'm going to have you start with your cell phone number, since there's no way I can know that in advance, and then we're going to randomize it from there," you say. "What's the area code of your cell phone number? 512? Okay, I don't want you to include the area code in these calculations. We're only going to use the primary seven digits. Fair enough?"

"Open up your calculator, and keep in mind that each time I give you a function, you need to complete it by hitting the 'equals' button. Start by putting the first three digits of your phone number in there. Great. Now multiply that number times eighty. Now add one, and then multiply the result by two hundred and fifty."

"So far, it's pretty random, right? Now I want you to add the last four digits of your phone number. And just to mix things up, add the last four digits a second time. Then subtract two hundred and fifty. What number did you come up with?"

Her number will be somewhere in the millions, and appear to be completely random. "Take a look at my prediction," you say. And as she opens the prediction, she discovers . . .

. . . a number that's nowhere near close to the result of her calculations.

"But that would have been cool, right?" you ask. "I mean, statistically, it's gotta work sometime."

. . . and at that exact moment, her phone rings.

And you're the one on the line.

Behind the Scam: Really, this one does itself: Just follow the steps and you'll end up with what appears to be a completely random number, but instead is exactly twice the value of her phone number.

FIRST 3 DIGITS
(×) 80
(+) 1
(×) 250
(+) Last 4
(+) Last 4

While she's looking at the prediction, all you need to do is divide her final result by two and you'll have her phone number. Since you already found out her area code, you can immediately call her number, or hold off for a big finish on a future trick later.

CHESS SCAMS

AUDIO COMMENTARY

bit.ly/1GblZpN

EPISODE ONE

bit.ly/1zsTDtL

EPISODE TWO

bit.ly/1Jl94EJ

IMPRESSIVENESS: 3/5-5/5

★ ★ ★ ★ ★

CLASS: CHESS CHALLENGES

FACTORS: IT'S CHESS...
WHICH CAN BE A PLUS OR MINUS.

REQUIRES: CHESSBOARDS
OR PEN AND PAPER

Oh man, were the episodes we did on chess scams polarizing. A lot of people wrote me to say these were the best tricks we'd taught to date, and others asked when we'd get back to the "good" stuff, like sticking nails in your nose.

Personally, I love these. And it was a blast to hang out with the Stanford Chess Club to learn them.

Play chess against 10 people at once . . . and win?

Imagine walking into a chess club and making this bold claim: "Grab ten of your very best players and set up ten chessboards. I'm going to play all ten of them simultaneously, and I'll bet you a thousand dollars that I'll win or tie at least half of the games."

You'd have to be some kind of chess genius to pull that off, right?

Actually . . . no. As long as you are familiar with the rules (and even that may not be necessary), you'll be able to make good on your claim.

Set up the 10 chessboards in a circle and play half the games as black, and half the games as white. Once all five white players have made their opening moves, mentally pair off each white player with a black one, and simply play them against each other.

You aren't making a single decision in the game. From now on, your job is simply to act as mail carrier between the various players. As long as you accurately recreate each move (which shouldn't be hard, since during tournament play all the moves are logged), you are absolutely guaranteed to win or tie at least half the games.

The Queen's Challenge:

This one sounds simple, but takes more effort than you'd think: Grab eight queens and an empty chessboard (you can use pawns and just pretend they're queens). Your challenge is to set all eight queens on the board in a configuration such that not one queen threatens another.

Before you look at the answer, give this one a try!

There are several variations, but the correct solution should look something like this:

Checkmate in one:

This one's easily my favorite. My friend and magician Curt Anderson completely stumped me with it, and only one person in the Stanford Chess Club was able to figure it out. To set this challenge up, place all the chess pieces in the entire game on the table, and set up the board as you see here:

"Chess rules have changed over the years, and some places have quirky house rules about promoting your pawn when it reaches the last row of the board. Just to be clear: in this challenge, you can promote your pawn to any piece in the entire game," you say.

"The challenge here is for white to checkmate in just one move."

Because there are so few pieces, your sucker will have the opportunity to try out every conceivable move for white before giving up and claiming it can't be done (and if you're up for the challenge, set up a board and give it a try yourself right now . . . I'll wait).

"Remember what I said in the beginning," you remind them. "I told you that a pawn could promote to any piece in the entire game." Which is why the solution is to promote white's pawn to a black knight!

I don't know if it's true or not, but Curt told me that until the 17th century there was no official rule that pawns couldn't promote to a piece of a different color. Allegedly, this problem was introduced as a reason to create the rule.

Part III:
LYING EYES

Think you can believe your eyes? Think again! These illusions will fool your marks while lining your pockets. Plus, you'll look -talented!-

CIRCUMFERENCE VS HEIGHT

IMPRESSIVENESS: 5/5

★ ★ ★ ★ ★

CLASS: CLOSER

FACTORS: FLAWED PERCEPTIONS

REQUIRES: ANY GLASS, A NAPKIN, STACKABLE ITEMS

AUDIO COMMENTARY

bit.ly/1JZwZdB

EPISODE

bit.ly/1dIeyQ9

This may be the single most useful scam we've ever taught: the illusion is utterly convincing, the reveal is satisfying, and the tools used can be found at any bar or restaurant. I've performed this hundreds of times, and it always impresses.

The Setup: Grab a glass, any glass. It can be a pint glass, a cocktail glass, or even a shot glass. Ask everyone at the table to take out a dollar, and then ask them which they think is longer: the circumference around the rim of the glass, or the height of the glass, from the table all the way up to the rim.

Make two piles with their dollars: one for people who say the circumference is longer and one for people who say height. You'll find the majority of people will say "circumference" at first (oh: and make sure to withhold your bet until the very end).

Next, place a pack of cigarettes (or a deck of cards) under the glass, and repeat the question. Now that it's obviously taller, a few of the players will now defect to the "height" side. Move their dollars over to the height pile. Then add another pack of cigarettes under the glass, and repeat.

Keep going round by round until the glass sits on a stack of cigarette packs and you're the only person left who will bet on circumference. Place your lone circumference bet, and then measure the circumference: grab a paper napkin, wrap it around the rim of the glass, and unwrap it to show that even with the extra added height, the circumference is still greater!

VIDEO DEMO

bit.ly/1zCxW5q

The Secret: People are just really, really bad at estimating circumferences. A pint glass is almost a foot around, but you'd never think it by looking at one. Before the trick, get an estimate of the circumference by wrapping your fingers around the rim of the glass. While you're adding supports underneath the glass, just make sure to stop right before the height matches the circumference.

Tip: If you want to actually make cash with this one, it's important to get everyone's money on the table. If they have a buck riding on it, they'll go with their true (wrong) estimates. If there's nothing at stake, I find that many people will keep saying "circumference" just to be contrary. You may actually find that your friends will need to put up $5 or $10 before they'll go with their guts.

LINKED CORKS

AUDIO COMMENTARY

bit.ly/1Gb2sbo

EPISODE

bit.ly/1dIeFuN

This one makes for a fantastic opener or conversation starter. It's quick, visual, surprising, and (best of all) it's just about impossible for people to duplicate the first time they see it.

The Setup: Place 2 wine corks in the crook of each of your thumbs, pinched against your index fingers.

The Goal: Transfer the cork in your left hand over to your right hand, and transfer the cork in your right hand over to your left hand.

corks swap hands, using only thumbs & index fingers

START

GOAL

The Twist: The swap must happen simultaneously, without using any other fingers and without tossing, balancing, or setting down of the corks.

When performed correctly, the end effect looks surprisingly like the two corks pass directly through each other.

This one's tough to put into words, so make sure to check out the video.

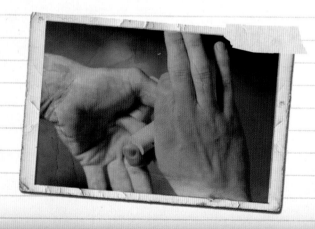

The Method: The trick is to over-rotate your right hand, placing the bottom side of your right thumb on the bottom of the left-hand's cork. Once you hit this first position, you'll notice that your left thumb and forefinger naturally rest on the top and bottom of the cork in your right hand. Finally, tilt your right hand forward so your right index finger rests on the top of the left hand's cork.

At this point you'll have an unusual grasp on both of the corks that will look like they're inter-linked, but you'll be able to pull them straight out from one another. The visual effect to most people will be seeing that you somehow pulled the corks straight through one another.

VIDEO DEMO

bit.ly/1OyDODG

This is the part where you clean up: offer to show them how it's done for a drink. Demonstrate slowly how its done, and then let them try to copy you. When they can't pull it off, offer them ANOTHER lesson . . . for another free drink!

CORK DROP

IMPRESSIVENESS: 3/5

★ ★ ★ ☆ ☆

CLASS: OPENER

FACTORS: SUPER SIMPLE,
SATISFYING MECHANIC

REQUIRES: WINE CORKS
(NATURAL OR SYNTHETIC)

AUDIO COMMENTARY

bit.ly/1O88jFx

EPISODE

bit.ly/1bWPL9G

This is a versatile little gem. Fun to do and visually interesting,
you can play it as a challenge for a free beer or simply teach it to
your friends.

The Setup: Grab some wine corks (either real or synthetic) and set up a simple challenge: from the height of at least one cork, drop your cork and have it land on one of its narrow, circular ends. To win the free beer (and to prove it's skill, not luck), you need to pull it off 2-3 times out of 10.

Sounds easy, right?

In fact, they don't have a chance. Just about everyone will drop the cork from a vertical position, and when it lands, it will bounce haphazardly.

To pull off the stunt, hold the cork horizontally, exactly one cork length above the table and release. When the cork hits (parallel to the table), it will bounce and twist just enough to land on its narrow, circular end! For synthetic corks, you'll need to drop them from a higher position. I've found that dropping synthetic corks from a height of one-and-a-half cork lengths is just about right.

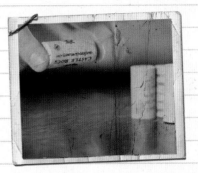

 VIDEO DEMO

bit.ly/1OyDRiC

toothpick
PULSE

AUDIO COMMENTARY

bit.ly/1JZx9lb

EPISODE

bit.ly/1GVAFyT

IMPRESSIVENESS: 2/5

★ ★ ☆ ☆ ☆

CLASS: TWEENER

FACTORS: FAKE TRICK, UNCOPYABLE

REQUIRES: WOODEN MATCHES OR FLAT-SIDED TOOTHPICK

Not sure how valuable this one is for scoring free beers, but it's a fun and simple conversation starter. Plus, you'll make your friends look like idiots.

How it Looks: You show your pulse using two toothpicks. No matter how hard they try, it never quite seems to work for your friends.

VIDEO DEMO #1

bit.ly/1E2djoE

How it's Done: Hold a toothpick horizontally by pinching one end between your thumb and forefinger, then laying it across the fingernail of your middle finger. Pull down with your index finger and push up against the toothpick with your middle fingernail. You should feel tension from the toothpick against your middle fingernail.

Next, lay a second toothpick on the first, so it balances on the palm of your hand and rests on the first toothpick.

If you press down and slide the first toothpick along your fingernail, the small ridges in your fingernail will cause the second toothpick to bounce wildly, seemingly without cause.

VIDEO DEMO #2

bit.ly/1blaTqy

By timing these movements, you'll be able to convince your friends that your pulse is causing the toothpick to move.

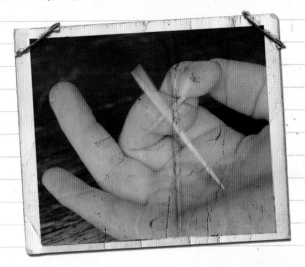

Now here's the important part: keep doing the trick like it's no big deal, explain to them how they should position the toothpicks, and act only mildly interested when they complain that they can't get it to work. This will drive them nuts! If you're looking to keep a girl pestering you for help the rest of the night, this is the effect for you.

I've noticed that it's much easier to do this effect with toothpicks that have a flat side. Round toothpicks have a tendency to roll right off, especially once they start bouncing around. If you can't find a square toothpick, try wooden matches.

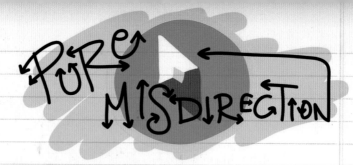

PURE MISDIRECTION

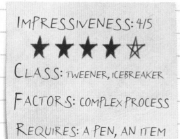

IMPRESSIVENESS: 4/5

★ ★ ★ ★ ☆

CLASS: TWEENER, ICEBREAKER

FACTORS: COMPLEX PROCESS

REQUIRES: A PEN, AN ITEM TO VANISH

AUDIO COMMENTARY

bit.ly/1yLh3uw

EPISODE

bit.ly/1Jl9URR

You're going to read this, and you're going to think there's no way this works.

You'll be wrong. I promise.

I first saw this on Michael Ammar's fantastic Icebreakers video set in the mid-90's, and I love the fact that this is an object lesson in the fundamentals of misdirection. Without using tricky moves, sleight of hand, or gimmicks of any kind, you're able to vanish a cork, coin, or any other small object. And you'll do it all using nothing but pure misdirection.

How it Looks: Grab a cork, salt-shaker top, or any object you can wrap your fingers around. With your other hand, hold a pen or straw as your "magic wand."

"Watch closely," you say, "because on the count of three, it's going to vanish." (Notice the careful phrasing here... it'll be important in a moment.)

Tap your fist slowly and deliberately with the pen three times, and on the third tap, the pen completely vanishes.

For about 5 seconds they'll be fooled, until you turn your head, point and reveal that the pen is nestled above your ear. After they groan, knock 'em dead: tap your fist three more times and open your hand to reveal the original object has completely vanished. It's not in your other hand ... it's completely gone.

How it's Done: As I mentioned, this one is all about misdirection. No need for any double joints or knuckle-busting skill, just the ability to focus your sucker's attention.

Plus, the work is even easier than you'd think: while you're setting up the first joke vanish, position your body to draw focus toward the cork. Hunch over and get them to look closely at your clenched fist. Remember: the tighter you can draw in their attention, the better this works.

Before each deliberate tap of the straw, pull the straw all the way up and into the crook of your ear. This consistency of motion will allow you to easily drop the straw before the third tap, and their hyperfocus on your closed fist will cause them to be fooled for a few seconds when the straw vanishes.

Now For the Important Part: At the exact moment they realize the straw is in your ear, their guard will be down and all their attention will be on your face. At this moment, completely relax your body and let your arms drop down. This will do two things:

1. Your relaxed disposition will cause them to relax as well. They'll assume you were just making a joke and the trick is over. In other words, your relaxation will cause them to temporarily drop their guard.
2. When you relax, you'll discover that the cork now rests mere inches from your pocket. Nobody's watching the cork, so . . .

At this moment, just deposit the cork into your pocket. No need to be tricky about it, they're not event going to be watching you by this point.

Before watching this demonstration, be warned: Since Michael Ammar is the one who taught this effect to me, I have elected to honor his legendary mustache by attempting to grow my own. The result is so hilariously awful, I had no choice but to use a time machine to go back and record this demonstration at a video arcade in the fall of 1984.

VIDEO DEMO

bit.ly/1cQPVAg

Now you're set. With the cork ditched, put your hand back into a closed fist as though you're still holding the cork. "Just kidding," you joke. "But seriously: wouldn't that be amazing if the cork did vanish?" Repeat the tapping motion, reveal your fist to be empty, and score your free drinks!

Will it FLOAT?

IMPRESSIVENESS: 3/5

★ ★ ★ ☆ ☆

CLASS: CLOSE

FACTORS: DEVELOPED SKILL

REQUIRES: METAL PAPER CLIPS, NAPKIN, CUP OR BOWL OF WATER

AUDIO COMMENTARY

bit.ly/1blaYKU

EPISODE

bit.ly/1dIf008

Sometimes you just need a few slam-dunk challenges – stuff that's not really about screwing anyone over, but just having a good time. This is one of those super-simple grandpa-type of challenges that's great to keep people occupied until you show them the surprisingly simple answer.

The Challenge: Place an all-metal paperclip into a glass of water, so that it floats on its own, supported only by the surface tension of the water's surface.

Their Attempts: Get ready for a lot of wet fingers. Most people will think it's simply a matter of finesse and continue to gingerly place the paper clip right on the surface, to no avail. (In

fact, once they get the paper clip and their fingers wet, it becomes just about impossible!)

Solution #1 (Elegant and Easy): Lay out a piece of napkin on the surface of the water, then simply drop the paper clip on top. The napkin will sink down on its own (or you can help it along with a little poking), and the paper clip will be left floating completely by itself!

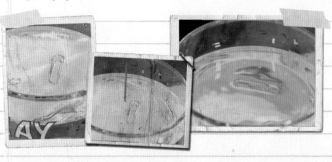

VIDEO DEMO (SMALL PAPER CLIP)

bit.ly/1E2dtfJ

Solution #2 (Harder and Uglier): Twist up one arm of the paperclip, so you can lower it onto the surface of the water without any part of your fingers breaking the seal of the water's surface. If performed delicately, you should be able to leave the paperclip straddling the water like a water bug.

Remember, though: Whenever you perform this, make sure you're using all-metal paper clips. If you use the ones coated in plastic, they may be light enough that a delicate hand could just drop them straight into the water.

One Additional Tip: Whichever method you use, make sure that each of the sharp ends is pointed up and away from the surface of the water. Otherwise, once one tip penetrates the water, capillary action will cause the rest of the paperclip to go sinking down.

# THROUGH the TABLE

IMPRESSIVENESS: 4/5

★★★★☆

CLASS: TWEENER

FACTORS: FUNDAMENTALS OF SLEIGHT-OF-HAND

REQUIRES: NAPKINS, SALT SHAKER, A COIN TO "VANISH"

AUDIO COMMENTARY

bit.ly/1GcX4qZ

EPISODE

bit.ly/1zsUSco

All right, so you learned the fundamentals of misdirection a couple of chapters back. Now we're going to combine those concepts with some tricky moves and an impromptu gimmick. The result will be a solid piece of magic theatre you can perform any time you're out to eat.

What it Looks Like: Claim you can send a coin penetrating right through the table, using only a salt shaker and a napkin. After an appropriate buildup, you'll instead slam your hand on the large salt shaker, appearing to vanish it down and through the table!

VIDEO DEMO

bit.ly/1GOyMeD

How it's Done: As I mentioned, this trick absolutely requires good misdirection (Don't sweat it though; it's easier than you think.) Start by putting all the focus on the coin to be vanished. Make it clear that the COIN is the focus. First, have it carefully examined and placed on the table. Next, grab a salt shaker and a napkin: wrap the napkin around the salt shaker, completely covering it. You can tap the shaker on the coin, and the glass will make a "clinking" sound to show that the coin is still there. Pull back the salt shaker a couple of times (to show nothing has happened yet), and during one of these "pull-backs," allow the shaker to drop down into your lap.

VIDEO DEMO (EXPOSED VIEW)

bit.ly/1JZxkgc

Now comes the acting: The napkin will retain the shape of the shaker, but you'll go on acting as though you're holding the actual object. Hold the (imaginary) shaker right over the coin, then slam your hand down, crushing the napkin and apparently sending the shaker right through the table. Wait a good 3-4 seconds for the effect to register with your audience, then pull out the shaker from under the table (actually from in your lap).

escape from a Straitjacket

IMPRESSIVENESS: 4/5

★ ★ ★ ★ ☆

CLASS: ESCAPE

FACTORS: PHYSICALLY DEMANDING, UNUSUAL RESTRAINTS

REQUIRES: STRAITJACKET

I love the straitjacket escape. It's been the finale of my touring stage show for over a decade now, and weirdly it's one of the few effects that's actually better when you know a bit about how it's done. Hell, when Houdini first started doing the straitjacket escape, he insisted on escaping behind a partition so nobody would know his secret techniques. But eventually he figured out that the drama of the escape was even better when the audience knew exactly what he was up to and could empathize with his struggle.

First, you should know that yes, there are such things as tricky, magicshop straitjackets. You can buy them at stores like Steven's Magic Emporium in Wichita, Kansas. I don't use one of those. I use fullyfunctional, ungimmicked units that come from the

Humane Restraint Company out of Madison, Wisconsin. They're the world's largest supplier of prison-grade humane restraints . . . and they have, without a doubt, the most awesomely terrifying catalog I've ever received.

(**Side note:** If you're a magician that uses one of those gimmicked jackets and you're totally pissed that I just told everyone that they exist, here's what you do: Tell everyone the exact same thing I just did. Hold your gimmicked straitjacket out right in front of them and boldly announce that some magicians use tricky jackets, but not you. You use a real straitjacket from the Humane Restraint Company. I swear on a stack of Tarbell's Course of Magic that nobody will ever, ever be able to see or care about the difference.)

When I first wanted to learn a straitjacket escape, the laws were a bit simpler: anyone was allowed to buy straitjackets direct from the manufacturer. However, in 1995, the FDA began to

regulate the sale of straitjackets (just like they do for prescription drugs) and it became illegal for anyone to buy them direct. The Humane Restraint Company wouldn't take my calls anymore, but luckily I found a medical reseller who didn't mind buying them on my behalf (as long as I paid a premium).

If you can't find one on the Internet (and seriously: how can anyone not find anything on the Internet?), then try hitting up a local tailor. There are plenty of designs to work from, and you can even get custom colors.

Once you've got the jacket, find a friend who doesn't mind strapping you in over . . . and over . . . and over. Because the short answer to the question of "how does a professional escape artist get out of a straitjacket?" is . . .

You wiggle. A lot. And once you've done it 300 times, you pretty much have the fundamentals figured out.

Now hang on: before you feel ripped off it's important to note that straitjackets are rarely designed to be "escape-proof." They're mainly used to prevent psychiatric patients from hurting themselves or others. As such, virtually no psychotics in a straitjacket will carefully think through the mechanics of the restraint, plan their process of escape, and then methodically flex their bodies in measured attempts to get free. If they have that level of self-control, they probably won't need the jacket.

If you ever watch this episode of Scam School, you'll get to see Dan Martin and me explain the mechanics of the escape with a see-through straitjacket. It's pretty cool. You'll see some tips on flexing your arms or grabbing extra slack while you're being strapped in. You'll learn that the first move should be to work your right arm over your head, followed by slipping your right elbow inside the sleeve. Next up, you'll sneak your hand down to the crotch strap, pinching it loose until it slides open . . . and finally you'll pull the jacket right off the top of your head like a sweater.

But all of that misses the point. Because those are just the mechanics of the escape, and it totally misses the magic.

The real secret to the straitjacket escape is to perform it ten thousand times. To perform it so often that you know every stitch of your jacket, the very limits of every muscle you flex. Perform it so often that you've figured out the exact right phrase to piss off your volunteers just enough so they pull as hard as they can on the crotch strap, locking you in so tight that the audience truly pities you.

In other words: become so confident in your ability to escape, that you intentionally make it as hard as possible on yourself. Because if you believe it's a challenge, the audience will as well.

Remember that escaping from a straitjacket isn't like picking a lock. It's like escaping from ropes. And how impressive a rope escape is depends entirely on how tightly the ropes are tied. Likewise for the straitjacket: the audience needs to believe it's legitimate, believe it's tight, and believe that the escape is for real stakes. And if you can make them believe, even for a few seconds, that live, on stage, you might actually fail . . .

Then you've learned the secret of the straitjacket escape.

SILVERWARE TRANSFORMATION

IMPRESSIVENESS: 1/5

ADORABLENESS: 4/5

★ ★ ★ ★ ☆

CLASS: CHEESY MAGIC TRICK

FACTORS: IT'S ADORABLE!
THAT'S ALL YOU NEED TO KNOW

REQUIRES: KNIFE, FORK,
LINEN NAPKIN

AUDIO COMMENTARY

bit.ly/1IxJ5ti

If there's one thing that Scam School has taught me, it's that people love learning just a little bit of magic. And whether you're performing this trick for little kids, or teaching it to a cutie at the bar, you're never worse off for knowing yet another fun diversion at the bar. No, this one's not rocket science, but it IS fun and cute.

The Effect: A fork is placed on a linen napkin, where it's rolled up, and then . . . BAM! Transforms into a knife! That's some crazy wizard powers, right there, right?! Where's my paycheck? And why are you not all screaming my name in adoration?? I just transformed a fork into a knife!! That's like, way better than the Philosopher's Stone! Religions have been started on less!

The Method: Before the trick, place a knife on the table and lay a linen napkin over it (make sure to leave folds and creases in the napkin to mask the shape of the knife).

Set the fork on top, and begin rolling the whole mess up into a linen burrito. Keep an eye on the edges of the linen napkin as it rolls around, and make sure to roll it far enough to send just one edge (or corner) over the top.

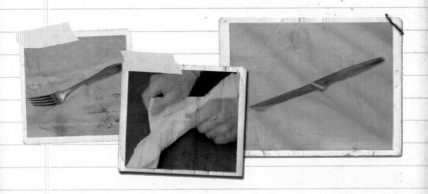

Now, when you pull apart the two corners to reveal the contents, they'll see the knife instead of the fork!

VIDEO DEMO

bit.ly/1blbd8D

VANISHING COIN trick

20¢4

IMPRESSIVENESS: 3/5

★ ★ ★ ☆ ☆

CLASS: TWEENER

FACTORS: BASIC SLEIGHT OF HAND

REQUIRES: 2 COINS, PRACTICE

AUDIO COMMENTARY

bit.ly/1EkhsGl

EPISODE

bit.ly/1GVBgAE

I met Daniel Martin the same day that I received the rough-cuts for the very first episodes of Scam School. Dan seemed to dig the show, and I was thrilled to have him appear on Scam School as often as we have.

Since Daniel Martin taught me this classic effect, I thought I'd give him the chance to teach it directly to you as well:

Daniel Martin here, invading the pages of the second Scam School book to bring you one of my favorite tricks to teach, which will even fool yourself when you perform it correctly!

How it Looks: Put a coin, beer cap, spider monkey . . . whateverunderneath each hand on a table and invisibly one of the objects travels to underneath the other hand! Boom . . . you're a witch!

How it's Done: The dirty secret is that it's all about how the coins are placed in your hands. If you place the 1st coin in the center of your palm (showing it to everyone) and turn your hand over quickly slamming it hand down on a table, the coin will stay put and remain directly underneath your hand! If you place the 2nd coin in the other hand, on the middle of your first two fingers (see photo) and turn your hand over quickly, the coin will shoot over to were your other palm side down hand is (speed & trajectory are kind of a big deal here).

So coin #1 stays put underneath your palm side down hand as you show it and turn your hand over. Coin #2 in the other hand, shoots over "invisibly" to where the other hand is! The key is the make it look as if both hands turn over at the same time, though in actuality the hand with coin #2 turns over a fraction of a second

quicker than the other hand with coin #1. This allows coin #2 to shoot over quickly & "invisibly" to make it underneath the hand with coin #1 before it's fully turned over so your hand can secretly cover both coins! The more you do it, the better it looks and the farther apart you can move your hands!

VIDEO DEMO

bit.ly/1cQQsC6

DM TIP: Remember, no one is supposed to see the other coin fly across the table underneath the other hand. After the dirty work is done, pause for a couple seconds, slide your hands around like you're a Brazilian masseuse, moving your hands farther apart like you're about to do something awesome . . . because you are! Enjoy it, use it, love it . . . thanks!

This one will take some practice, but once you have the knack down, it'll look killer.

floating "—" "MATCH HEADS"

IMPRESSIVENESS: 4/5

★ ★ ★ ★ ☆

CLASS: CLOSER

FACTORS: SCIENCE

REQUIRES: MATCH HEADS, BOTTLE, WATER

AUDIO COMMENTARY

bit.ly/1cQQtGn

EPISODE

bit.ly/1R6qoTk

This one's fun because you can perform it as a quickie illusion or as a bet to score yourself a free drink.

Before You Start: Fill an empty beer bottle (preferably clear) all the way to the top with water, then grab 3 wooden matches and break off the heads (make sure to break them off as close to the actual match head as possible).

Next, announce that you're going to place all three match heads in the bottle and cover it up with your thumb . . .

The Question is: Does your friend think the match heads will sink or float?

Amazingly, it doesn't matter what their answer is, because you'll counter with the following prediction:

"I think one match head will sink, one will float, and one will suspend itself, floating in the center of the glass."

It sounds crazy, right? Yet, after you drop the match heads into the bottle and cover the top with your thumb, something amazing will happen: At first, they'll float right at the top, but as you press down with your thumb to increase the internal pressure, one match head will sink to the bottom, another will remain floating at the top, and the third will drop exactly halfway down the bottle, suspending itself in place!

VIDEO DEMO

bit.ly/1HM5y7V

So What's Happening? When you break off the match heads, you're actually creating miniature "Cartesian divers"... little vessels with air trapped in them. As the pressure increases, the air

compresses and makes them heavier than the water. Once you've dropped the match heads in the bottle, just use your thumb to make a tight seal and press down into the bottle.

This will increase the pressure and allow you to imperceptibly control the height of the match heads inside the bottle!

If you don't have a glass bottle or match heads, you can make an impromptu ketchup packet and a plastic water bottle. It'll be easier to squeeze, and have the exact same effect.

(Big thanks to friend of the show Diamond Jim Tyler for suggesting this impromptu variation.)

SEEING STARS

IMPRESSIVENESS: 2/5

★ ★ ☆ ☆ ☆

CLASS: TWEENER

FACTORS: EXTREMELY
SLOW PAYOFF

REQUIRES: TOOTHPICKS
OR MATCHES

AUDIO COMMENTARY

bit.ly/1D7ryEK

This isn't a scam. It's got no sucker-punch payoff. Nobody
will feel like an idiot when it's over. You won't collect a fat reward.
You won't earn a free beer.

So you're asking "Why do I want to learn it, then?"

Why? Because it's a sweet little visual treat, and you're going
to make someone happy.

Sure, this is a grandpa-style magic trick, but at some point
you're going to find yourself sitting at a table with a beautiful girl
who just wants to see something cute and fun. And then you'll
thank me for teaching you this one.

The Work: Grab 5 wooden matches or toothpicks, and break
them in half. Don't completely break them apart, but instead make

sure that each one still has strong connective wood between each half. Set them up to look like a big asterisk, like so:

Next, dribble a bit of water on the center of the matches (make sure you do so slowly, so as not to disturb their positions).

Finally: wait. And keep waiting.

VIDEO DEMO

bit.ly/1QajonW

At first, you won't see anything . . . but slowly and surely over the next 15 minutes, the water will be absorbed into the matchsticks. And as the water is absorbed, the wood will expand, and the matches will start to straighten themselves out. After several minutes, you'll have a perfectly formed 5-point star!

BRAIN-MELTING
COIN ILLUSIONS

AUDIO COMMENTARY

bit.ly/1JmBKgi

EPISODE

bit.ly/1cdBjLj

IMPRESSIVENESS: 4/5

★ ★ ★ ★ ☆

CLASS: CLOSER

FACTORS: PERCEPTION TRICKS

REQUIRES: LOTS OF RANDOM COINS

Oh, man, do I love these illusions ... and I wish I could take credit for discovering them. Both of these came to me from my friend Diamond Jim Tyler, who published them in his book Bamboozlers. They're both fantastic, and you'll totally fool yourself.

The Stack: Place 10 quarters in a stack and place them on some kind of pedestal (like your cell phone or a deck of cards). In front of this stack, place on the table (in order) a 50-cent piece, a quarter, a nickel, a penny, and a dime.

Ask your mark which coin, when placed on its side, will be as tall as the stack of quarters. Almost everyone will pick the nickel or quarter, but you'll blow them away when you reach over and show them it's the DIME that's just as tall!

Half dollar - quarter - nickel - penny - dime

We've already learned from the circumference vs. height scam that we're all bad at translating horizontal lengths into vertical ones. To really make this trick work for you, it's important that you include that fiftycent piece in the row of coins. It's such a big coin that it completely throws off your sense of scale for all the others. Try it for yourself!

10 QUARTERS VIDEO DEMO

bit.ly/1zCyl7K

The Drip: Grab the nickel from the previous scam and ask them to guess "how many drops of water I can place on this nickel before the water overflows?"

Most will pick 3-5.

Some may say 5-10.

A real wise-ass will pick 15.

But NOBODY will pick the real answer, which will amazingly be well over twenty drops!

WATER DROPS ON NICKEL DEMO

bit.ly/1H8roTP

DIMES IN A SHOT GLASS

AUDIO COMMENTARY

bit.ly/1G0z19m

EPISODE

bit.ly/1ELx3vI

IMPRESSIVENESS: 4/5
★★★★☆
CLASS: CLOSER
FACTORS: VISUALLY IMPRESSIVE PAYOFF
REQUIRES: SHOT GLASS AND A LOT OF DIMES

Here's another one that takes advantage of flawed perceptions. Don't underestimate its power . . . LEST IT DESTROY YOU!!!

Before You Start: Fill a shot glass all the way to the rim with water. Swap a five-dollar bill for a fistful of dimes, then ask your friend "How many dimes do you think can be carefully dropped into this shot glass before the first drop trickles over the edge?"

They'll say: Something like 5. Maybe 10. 15, if they really want to mess with you. Regardless of what they say, make sure you get them to firmly commit to their predictions before you write down (and hide) your own prediction.

The Experiment: There's no trickery here . . . just carefully drop dimes into the shot glass, and watch their amazement as you pass 15 dimes . . . then 20 dimes . . . and even more!

In a standard shot glass, I'm usually able to put 22-25 dimes in before it overflows. And you can put in even more if you cheat: each time you place a dime in the water, let it barely touch your fingers. You'll be sneakily pulling water out of the glass and allowing for many more dimes.

If you want to set this up as a side-by-side bet of skill, just make sure you sneak just the tiniest amount of soap onto his shot glass. It'll reduce the amount of surface tension, and he won't have a prayer of keeping up with you.

VIDEO DEMO

bit.ly/1F7rx8o

Part IV:
DIRTY TRICKS

A dash of nasty pranks... What's not to love? Just use discretion on these, and don't get us into any trouble.

KUNG FU MATCH TRAP

AUDIO COMMENTARY

bit.ly/1Gb31Sv

EPISODE

bit.ly/1EODbOH

IMPRESSIVENESS: 5/5

★ ★ ★ ★ ★

CLASS: NASTY PRANK

FACTORS: PHYSICAL INJURY, DANGER, FIRE

REQUIRES: BOX OF MATCHES, THE RIGHT KIND OF MARK

A while back I got an email from "Cowboy" in the UK, a longtime fan and contributor to Scam School. In it was the most insidious, diabolical, genius, and EVIL bar trick I've ever seen.

I've loved this one since the moment I first tried it, but be warned: you'll need to be very careful choosing whom you perform this on.

Get a box of matches that has striking surfaces on each side. Pull out three matches, and have your victim hold two of them (match-head side down) pinched against each side of the matchbox. Balance the third match across the tops of the two pinched matches.

The Challenge: Promise your friend that you'll buy him a beer if he can "karate chop" the balanced match, using just one finger. If he can break that top match in two without it falling off the side-posts, a tall, frosty one awaits . . . and he doesn't even need to bet anything of his in return! What could be more fair?

The Blow-off: It won't matter if he pulls it off or not, because the moment he strikes at the top match, the downward force will cause one (or both) of the pinched matches to strike!

Even better, after pinching them for so long, he'll find that the burning match is stuck to his thumb or forefinger!

VIDEO DEMO

bit.ly/1blbQ27

Warning: you will absolutely burn your victim pulling this trick. Plus, he may fling a burning match into someplace highly flammable. At the very least, you will owe your friend/enemy a beer, and at the very worst, you will burn down the bar and get your ass kicked.

So . . . use this one with caution. And adult supervision. And make sure it's a cautious adult that's supervising you. In fact, now that I think about it . . . you probably should never do this one. Forget that you ever saw it.

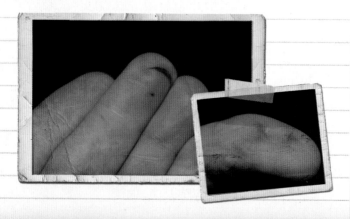

THE TIP-OVER BOX

AUDIO COMMENTARY

bit.ly/1IxJImI

EPISODE

bit.ly/1bskISw

IMPRESSIVENESS: 2/5

★ ★ ☆ ☆ ☆

CLASS: TWEENER

FACTORS: EXTREMELY SIMPLE, EASY

REQUIRES: MATCHBOX

This short and sweet scam is perfect in so many ways: you can do it anytime, anywhere, with an item you'll find at most bars, and best of all: it's a totally rigged game that lets you decide who wins and who loses.

The prop couldn't be simpler: just find an empty matchbox that has the same design on both sides. Set it on the table with the inside tray facing up (we'll call that "right-side-up") and start making a simple game of balancing the box with one side on the edge of the table and the other on your fingertip.

The challenge is to bring up your hand slowly enough that when the box reaches the vertical position, it stands erect without tipping over. It's okay if you flub the first couple of tries (it genuinely is a minor challenge), but eventually get it right and declare yourself "Awesome."

Once you've done it a few times, your mark should be interested in giving it a go himself. Explain the rules, and set it up the same way for him. First try, he'll probably get it (and not see what's so hard about it). Perfect. Once he has won a couple of times in a row, tell him he's only got beginner's luck, and bet him a beer that he can't do it three times in a row.

Once he agrees, set up the box "right-side-up" for the first two tries, but for the third one, flip it with the internal tray upside-down.

The box won't look any different, but this time, when he raises his fingers up, the distribution of weight inside the matchbox will make it impossible for him to win.

bit.ly/1Gb35BF

Seriously: try it yourself. Every single time, the box will overcompensate and fall forward, guaranteeing you a free tasty beverage.

Special thanks to Todd Robbins for featuring this gem in his book Modern Con Man, giving us permission to use it on Scam School, and for writing one of the nicest, most confidence-building emails I've ever received.

BANG YOUR HEAD

IMPRESSIVENESS: 4/5

★ ★ ★ ★ ☆

CLASS: NASTY PRANK

FACTORS: INSULT, INJURY, HILARITY

REQUIRES: WILLING VICTIM, A COIN, GUTS

Out of all the effects we've done on Scam School, this is the one I was most skeptical would actually work. As an experiment, I made a habit of trying it on as many people as I could . . . and not one person figured it out. Hell, I saw one guy nearly knock himself out trying this one!

So be careful with this. Use it with discretion, and realize after this trick, you owe them a beer.

How it Looks: Your friend beats his head on the bar repeatedly, to everyone's delight.

How it's Done: I'm serious, guys . . . be careful with how far you take this one. It could get nasty.

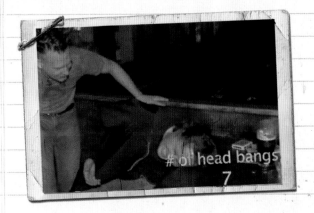

Explain to your friend that there's a peculiar attribute of physics that makes a coin rather difficult to remove from your forehead. Demonstrate this for him by taking a quarter and using your thumb to press and stick it to your forehead. Now tilt your head to the right and lightly bang down on the bar. "See," you say, "the force of the banging is all downward, so it takes two or three good whacks to get the coin off." And sure enough, after a few more whacks, the coin falls off your head and down onto the table.

Here's where it gets good: If you've sold the novelty well enough, your friend will accept the challenge to try it himself (it helps to promise him a beer if he can do it in fewer than five whacks). Take the quarter and push it for 3 to 5 seconds against his forehead, but make sure your fingernails are wrapped around the edges of the coin. This will allow you to remove the coin as you move your hand away. Amazingly, if you pressed hard, your friend won't be able to tell that the coin is no longer on his forehead!

Now, have your friend do just like you did, and bang his head on the bar until his coin falls off. Of course, he'll keep on banging since there's no coin to knock off. The game ends when he injures himself or figures out there's no coin on his head, whichever comes first.

LEVERAGE!

AUDIO COMMENTARY

bit.ly/1DtLvF3

EPISODE

bit.ly/1GVD7FE

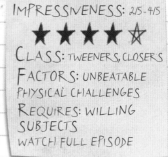

IMPRESSIVENESS: 2/5 - 4/5

★ ★ ★ ★ ☆

CLASS: TWEENERS, CLOSERS
FACTORS: UNBEATABLE
PHYSICAL CHALLENGES
REQUIRES: WILLING
SUBJECTS
WATCH FULL EPISODE

Here are three surprising ways to use leverage to make your friends look dumb, and one of them actually creates a magic moment for the sucker as well:

Punk #1 Setup: Have your friend put his left cheek and the side of his left shoe up against a wall. Under his right foot, place a $20 bill.

The Challenge: Without holding on to anything, (and without letting go of the wall), challenge him to lift his right foot off the bill for 6 seconds . . . he won't be able to do it!

It makes sense from a weight-distribution standpoint: because he can never push his body past the wall, he'll never equalize out his center of gravity, which means any time he lifts his foot, he'll topple right over.

Just make sure he doesn't try to sneakily grab on to the wall or twist his foot sideways. Keep him honest, and there's no chance.

Punk #2 Setup: With his butt and the backs of his heels placed firmly against the wall, place a $20 bill on his shoes.

The Challenge: Without bending at the knees, he need only bend over and pick up the $20. If he can do it without falling over, it's his. But remember: No butt sliding or crazy dance moves! He has to simply bend over at the waist and pick it up.

He might be able to reach over and pick it up, but will definitely be falling forward afterward.

Punk #3 Setup: This one is my favorite, as you'll actually create an ever-so-brief feeling that he's just been hypnotized.

Have your friend sit relaxed in a chair with no arms. He should be slouched with his feet outward. Announce you're about to hypnotize him, and start doing some nutty ritual: dance around, stare intently into his eyes, repeat a creepy poem five times . . . you name it. But at the end of your ritual, place your thumb gently on his forehead, and tell him that he's just been hypnotized.

The Challenge: Explain that your thumb is now made of iron, and he's powerless to resist even your very slight pressure. To prove it, tell him try to stand up; because he has no leverage, you'll find it hilariously easy to keep him stuck in his chair using only one finger.

And best of all: for that one, brief second in the moment he first tries to stand up, your thumb will go from feeling like the softest touch to a completely immovable object. That moment of transformation will, for the briefest of moments, actually feel like magic to them.

●

AUDIO COMMENTARY

bit.ly/1EkiYZa

EPISODE

bit.ly/1JM48w6

IMPRESSIVENESS: 3/5

★ ★ ★ ☆ ☆

CLASS: PRANK (WITH TRICK ENDING)

FACTORS: ANNOY THE MARK!

REQUIRES: STACK OF BAR NAPKINS

Andrew Mayne is a genius. Also: a jerk.

When I first invited him on Scam School, I didn't want to know what he was going to perform . . . I wanted the experience for me to be totally fresh, as I knew whatever he'd come up with would be amazing, wellthought, and fun.

What I didn't expect was that I'd get chumped and fooled on my own show. Here's what he put together for us:

The Setup: Challenge your friend to stuff as many napkins in his mouth as possible (while still being safe). Before they begin, promise you're going to make a prediction of what the final number will be by sending your friend a text (which he can verify has arrived either by tone or vibration . . . but don't let them see it in advance!).

With his phone face down on the table, let him run wild and stuff as many as he possibly can. Start cheering for him. Egg him on. Hell, start helping him by wadding up napkins for him to stuff his face with . . .

The Suckerpunch: When he hits his absolute limit, when he can't possibly get one more napkin in there, when he finally calls "uncle," take note of how many napkins he ended up with in his mouth.

Then, with a knowing smile and a grand flourish, reveal your texted prediction: "You will have a very dry mouth."

The Twist: He'll be pissed and feel like a fool, but his annoyance will turn to amazement when you turn over the very next napkin to reveal your real handwritten prediction:

"You will stop at number 27."

. . . the exact number he stopped on!

The Work: The first part is a nasty prank, but it also serves an important function of acting as a red herring. Because the sucker thinks the prediction is on the phone, he'll pay no attention to the napkins he's stuffing in his face. And because of that, he'll never notice that each of the napkins he's eating has another prediction written on its back.

That's right: to set up this scam, simply label the 10th through 30th napkins with "you will stop on 23," "you will stop on 24," etc., and place them back in the stack in order.

After he's gone through the first 10 napkins, that's when you start picking them up and wadding them up as you push them into his mouth. That way there's no chance for him to see the other predictions.

To cover your tracks, when you get to the end, hold the final napkin in one hand, while flipping over the full stack in the other.

That way, when they see the prediction, they'll also see that it's the only one in the stack labeled that way!

For more ingenious tricks and deception, check out Andrew Mayne's website at andrewmayne.com, and make sure to check out the weird things podcast featuring Me, Andrew, and Justin Robert Young at weirdthings.com

MAGIC $BILL$
SHORT CON

AUDIO COMMENTARY

bit.ly/1E2gOLy

EPISODE

bit.ly/1GUUvY8

IMPRESSIVENESS: 4/5

★ ★ ★ ★ ☆

CLASS: TWEENER (ALSO: CRIME)
FACTORS: IMPRESSIVE TRICK THAT'S DEFINITELY STEALING
REQUIRES: SECRET ACCOMPLICE

This one is part magic trick, part street con, and all illegal:

What They See: Imagine you're at a bar, and a likeable patron offers to perform an absolutely unbelievable magic trick: A $100 bill is taken from the register. The bartender writes his name clearly and boldly across the face. Our magician crumples up the bill, wraps it in a cocktail napkin, drops it in a wine glass, and drops a match in. The bill is consumed in flames and immediately becomes ashes. The performer does some gestures, and then points to the register, 20 feet down the bar. To everyone's surprise, the signed $100 bill is IN THE REGISTER! The magician is a hero, and the bartender buys a round of drinks on the house.

The Scam: The magician got much more than a round of drinks out of the deal. Under cover of wadding up the bill, the magician-turned-con man switches the $100 for a $1, handing off the $100 to a friend. While the magician is putting on a show, his accomplice walks down to the end of the bar, orders two drinks, and pays with the $100 bill. Not only does this put the magic bill back in the register, but the accomplice walks away with $90 change on the bar's own $100!

When we planned to do this one on Scam School, I knew the magic would fool the bartender, but I didn't know if she'd pick up on the fact that we had actually stolen some of the bar's money. To my surprise, she was utterly fooled, and more importantly: it never even occurred to her to be on guard against an attempt at fraud.

That's the genius of this scam: The bartender sees a very simple trick. The hundred is taken from the register; the hundred returns to the register. Case closed. The only way for the bartender to even be suspicious is if he learns how the trick is done.

Quick note on this scam: I got an email from some folks who told me that they've actually been doing this trick at bars. I reminded them (as I remind you) that actually pulling this trick as described is a genuine crime.

Speaking of which, I think one of the best explanations we've given for this trick was when Fox7 news in Austin asked me to break down a couple of bar scams, including this one and the short change.

Check it out:

SCAM SCHOOL ON FOX-7 NEWS

bit.ly/1DELRs3

Part V:

CARD TRICKS!

(THAT TOTALLY DON'T SUCK)

Everyone needs to know a couple of really awesome card tricks. It's the law. (and you know that we're all about obeying the law here at Scam School.)

CONTROLLED CARDS

AUDIO COMMENTARY

bit.ly/1yLixF6

EPISODE

bit.ly/1dIhMDb

IMPRESSIVENESS: 3/5-5/5

★ ★ ★ ★ ★

CLASS: FUNDAMENTAL SLEIGHTS

FACTORS: IMPORTANT UTILITY MOVES FOR ALL CARD TRICKS

REQUIRES: CARDS, PRACTICE

The Scam School books are fantastic at teaching you how to scam, swindle, and steal . . . but we don't seem to be big on the "giving you actual talent" thing.

Good news: that all changes in this chapter. We're going to learn not only how to control a card to the bottom of the deck, but how to combine that talent with a basic card force to make a sweet little trick! They'll pick a card, and everything will be fairly shuffled; yet amazingly, they'll cut the deck to their own exact card!

Prerequisites: The Overhand Shuffle

First thing you need to do is learn how to perform a basic overhand shuffle. You can Google it (or just watch the videos

throughout the section), but the basic mechanics are incredibly simple: Hold the deck as a block in your right hand and use your left hand to peel off cards, 3 to 7 of them at a time.

Overhand shuffling used to be the most popular form of shuffling (think back to the days of riverboat casinos), until it became clear that it was way too easy to manipulate the order of the deck . . . which is exactly what you're about to do.

Part 1: Controlling a Card to the Bottom

Once you know how to do the overhand shuffle, you know that part of the shuffle includes pulling a few cards off the top of the deck over and over again. To control a card from the top of the deck down to the bottom, start with a couple of regular overhand shuffles. Once you're finished, have him place his card on top of the deck.

Now here's the important part: instead of pulling off a random number of cards, make sure you peel off exactly one. This will place his card as the first in your left hand, and from now on you can shuffle normally. No matter what you do through this first round of shuffling, his card will now be on the bottom of the deck.

TOP TO BOTTOM DEMO

bit.ly/1DtNBol

Part 2: Keeping his Card at the Bottom

This one's only slightly trickier: when you begin your second round of shuffling, pinch the top and bottom cards of the deck with

your left hand, and with your right hand pull the entire deck of cards out from the middle. If executed correctly, this will allow you to pull out almost all the cards of the deck, leaving only the top and bottom cards in your left hand. More importantly, as you continue to shuffle, the bottom card will remain on the bottom of the deck.

The best part? You can keep repeating this move as many times as you like, and shuffle as sloppily as you like. Everything will look totally fair, and no matter what you do, his card will remain at the bottom of the deck.

MAINTAIN ON BOTTOM DEMO

bit.ly/1Ho5s5D

Part 3: The Reveal

So you've got the mark's card on the bottom of the deck. Now the challenge is to reveal it in a surprising manner.

Holding the cards in your hand, ask the mark to cut off as many cards as they like and place them on the table. This part is 100% fair, and they really can cut the deck anywhere they like.

Once they've placed half the deck on the table, "mark" their cut by laying the leftover cards from your hand "cross-ways" over the cards on the table, forming an "X." At this point, the controlled card (the one that was on the bottom of the deck) will be on the bottom of the upper pack of cards.

Take a few seconds to recap how you got here: "You had a free choice of card, right? You saw me shuffle the deck repeatedly, right? Finally, you chose where to cut the cards, right?" This time delay is an important part of pulling off the illusion, and is easier than it sounds.

Finally, turn over the top packet of cards and reveal that they randomly cut to their own card.

Magicians call this last move the "crisscross force," and it can be used either to pre-determine a "randomly selected" card, or as a novel way for them to find their own card.

Part 4: Alternate Endings

Let's say you'd rather have the selected card appear on the other half of the crisscross force . . . or better yet, you've cooked up your own ending that requires their card to be on top of the deck instead of the bottom. In either case, you'll need to bring their card up to the top of the pack using these moves:

Start by overhand shuffling cards as you normally would from your right hand into your left hand. As you near the end of the deck of cards, begin using your left thumb to peel cards off from your right hand just one at a time. As long as you're pulling cards off exactly one at a time, you're guaranteed to end up with the last card of the deck on top.

BOTTOM TO TOP DEMO

bit.ly/1O8b9Kz

Even Better: If you want to look like a total sleight of hand wizard, combine the moves you learned above with the one-handed cut you learned from Scam School Book 1:

Follow the exact same moves to have a card selected, shuffled and "lost" in the pack (actually just kept at the bottom of the deck). Then for your big reveal, start to execute the one-handed cut, but perform this variation when you'd normally let the top half of the deck fall on the bottom half:

Instead of letting the top part of the deck fall flush, have it fall onto your middle finger, then roll forward the tip of your middle finger to drag the bottom-most card out of the deck. Once you have

it out past the halfway point, continue to roll it around the side of the deck to deposit it face up on the top.

To your target, it will look as though you just happened to cut the deck to the right card, and pulled it out of the deck . . . all using just one hand.

SPREAD DEMO

bit.ly/1O8bcWZ

THE VANISHING CARD TRICK

AUDIO COMMENTARY

bit.ly/1GcZHZW

EPISODE

bit.ly/1ERQyUG

IMPRESSIVENESS: 4/5

★ ★ ★ ★ ☆

CLASS: TWEENER

FACTORS: ADVANCE PREP WORK

REQUIRES: DECK OF CARDS, DOUBLE-SIDED TAPE

More fundamentals, here: you'll learn another tricky shuffle, a card force, and a method for a simple card vanish.

The Effect: A card is randomly selected, vanishes from the deck, and appears inside your freakin' shoe!

The Pre-Set: This one's a really killer effect, but it takes just a little bit of work to set up properly. Start by grabbing a face card (I used the jack of hearts) and placing some double-sided tape over the busy part of the design. The visual noise on the card will make the tape virtually impossible to detect, and the tape makes the vanish possible.

Place this card on the bottom of the deck and a stick a duplicate of the same card (from another pack) inside your shoe, and you're ready to go.

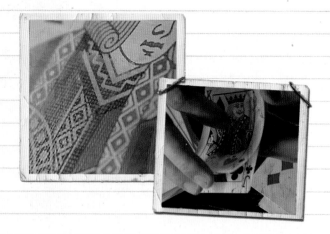

The Force: To "freely select" the card you've prepared, hold the pack from the above with the fingers of your right hand on each of the long sides of the deck. Start running through the cards, pulling packets of cards off the top of the deck and allowing them to drop into a stack in the palm of your left hand (this type of shuffle is called the "Hindu shuffle" and will take just a little bit of practice. Watch the video and you should get it down quickly).

When your mark says "stop," confirm that he's certain of his choice, and then show him the bottom card of the deck (the one with your doublesided tape). Even though you're just showing the bottom card of the deck, he'll have the firm impression that you're showing him a completely random card he chose to stop on. After he's got his card memorized, drop all the cards from your right hand back onto the pack (sticking your gimmicked face card onto the next card down).

VIDEO DEMO

bit.ly/1H8tHpX

The Vanish: Next, ask them what card they selected (as if you didn't know its your prepared face card). When they answer, announce that just like that you've teleported it out of the deck. Prove that it's gone by spreading all the cards on the table and showing the card is completely missing from the deck. (It's actually in there, but stuck to another random card ... it's shockingly undetectable.)

And finally . . .

The Reveal: Pull off your shoe, reach inside, and pull out their selected card!

Even if you don't want to prepare your cards with the double-sided tape, it's worth learning this trick just for the tricky shuffle. (You'll need it to perform "Scorched" in a few chapters.) Not only is it a legitimate shuffle, but an awesome way to force any card, making possible any number of magic tricks of your own creation.

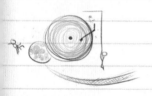

the HOT SEAT
card trick

AUDIO COMMENTARY

bit.ly/1J2U2Xa

EPISODE

bit.ly/1K8lSOK

IMPRESSIVENESS: 5/5

★ ★ ★ ★ ★

CLASS: TWEENER

FACTORS: PRE-SET, SPECIAL EQUIPMENT

REQUIRES: FRIXION BRAND PEN, CARDS, CANDLE

Steve Daly is awesome. And funny. And talented. He was a consultant on Criss Angel's Mindfreak, and he first showed me this trick at a magic convention in Dallas several years ago. I was thrilled when he offered to let us teach this on Scam School.

How it Looks: The scammer pulls out a deck of cards, shuffles them, and produces a previously-written prediction from his pocket. Cards are handed to the sucker, who picks a secret number between 10 and 20 and deals down that many cards onto the table.

These cards are picked up, and to make things even MORE random, the sucker is asked to add up the digits of his first number (for example, if it was 13, he'd add 1+3=4), and deal down that many cards.

Once finished, the sucker flips over the final card dealt, which is revealed to be the three of clubs.

VIDEO DEMO

bit.ly/1EkjdmR

Triumphantly, the scammer opens his prediction and reveals that before the trick even began, he knew the chosen card would be . . .

. . . the eight of spades.

Crestfallen, our hero looks around for a way to salvage his performance. "Aha!" he says as he grabs a cocktail candle from the table. "Watch," he says, as he waves the prediction over the flame . . . And visibly, right before everyone's eyes, his prediction transforms from the eight of spades to the three of clubs!

The Work: To pull this one off, you'll need to get a Frixion pen from Pilot. These pens use "erasable ink" that turns invisible

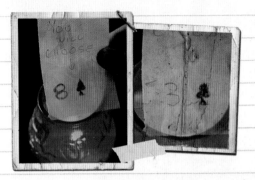

whenever it heats up. Normally you'd use the eraser of the pen to provide enough friction to heat up the ink, but in our case we'll use the candle for a stunning visual transformation.

With a normal ballpoint pen, write out: "You will pick the 3 of ♠." Then use the Frixion pen to draw over the number and suit, so it appears to read: "You will pick the 8 of ♠." Fold the prediction in half and place it on the table.

WRITING DEMO

bit.ly/1cQUc6T

Next, pre-set the deck so the three of clubs is the 10th card down. You can shuffle the deck all you want; just don't disturb those top 10 cards.

Once the trick begins, it doesn't matter what number between 10 and 20 your sucker chooses. The added step of having him also deal down the number of cards equal to the sum of both digits will guarantee that you always end up at the tenth card down in the deck, which you already know will be the 3 of clubs.

As you get closer to revealing your prediction, make sure to really pour on the smug self-confidence. The more smug you are, the happier they'll be to see you fail. And the more amazed they'll be when you magically correct your mistake!

TRICK REVEAL DEMO

bit.ly/1zCzLzg

Keep in mind this principle can be used for much more than just card tricks. You can set up jokes, secret messages, you name it. Get creative and let me know what you come up with.

YOU DO AS I DO

IMPRESSIVENESS: 3/5

★ ★ ★ ☆ ☆

CLASS: TWEENER

FACTORS: PROCEDURAL INSTRUCTIONS

REQUIRES: 2 DECKS OF CARDS

AUDIO COMMENTARY

bit.ly/1blefcW

EPISODE

bit.ly/1GVDIXJ

In this trick, you'll create an unbelievable coincidence . . . and you won't even have to learn any new moves!

What They See: Grab two decks of cards. You hold one, and the sucker holds the other. Both of you shuffle your cards until you're both certain that neither of you could possibly know the order of any of the cards.

To make sure there's no funny business, you even swap decks. Then each of you pulls out a random card in your respective decks, set it on top, and complete the cut (making sure to remember your card). Finally, each of you takes back your original deck, looks through the cards, and pulls out the card

you selected earlier. On the count of three, each of you turns over your cards to reveal that, incredibly, both of you picked the exact same card!

The Method: While this looks like a completely new effect, you're actually using the exact same method as the Key Card trick you learned in the first *Scam School* book.

Follow all the process exactly as detailed above, only before you swap decks, make sure to note the bottom card in your deck (that's going to be your "key card"). When each of you pulls out a

random card, pay no attention to the card you're actually selecting, but instead keep thinking of your key card. Meanwhile, over on your sucker's deck, the action of completing the cut will place his card directly beneath your key card.

Finally, when you take back your original deck, run through the cards, locate your key, and then pull out the card underneath it. Set it down as if it was the card you originally selected at random, and when both of you flip over your "selected cards," you've got a miraculous coincidence!

Memorize A Deck of Cards in Seconds!

AUDIO COMMENTARY

bit.ly/1zCzRHd

EPISODE

bit.ly/1dIidgD

IMPRESSIVENESS: 4/5

★ ★ ★ ★ ☆

CLASS: TWEENER

FACTORS: MIX OF SKILL AND FRAUD

REQUIRES: DECK OF CARDS

I cooked up this trick almost 20 years ago and still use it today to fool magicians. Everything about it just screams "totally fair," but the best part is it uses a principle that every magician knows (but won't suspect).

What They See: Grab a deck of cards and have them fully shuffled. Have a card picked at random, placed on top, then cut into the deck. Finally, give the deck one solid riffle shuffle.

Fair enough?

Next, spread out the entire deck and announce you're going to memorize the order of the entire deck in just 10 seconds. Slowly run your finger as you look from one end of the spread cards to the other.

"Got it!" you finally announce. "Now to prove my point, I'm going to turn around, and I want you to remove your card and replace it somewhere completely different in the deck."

Once they've done as you ask, have them square up the deck and leave it on the table. Turn back around and spread the cards again.

"Let's see," you begin. "If you followed my instructions, every single card in the deck should be unchanged . . . except for . . . Aha! This one's in the completely wrong spot!" you exclaim, tossing their card right in front of them.

What You Do: Amazingly, you use not one, but two key cards. By sandwiching their card between two key cards, it becomes possible to give the deck one good riffle shuffle, and completely convince magicians that there's no chance you're using the key card principle.

When you spread out the cards, immediately look for your two key cards. There will be anywhere from two to five cards in-between them, one of which is their selected card. The entire time you're pretending to memorize the deck, instead memorize just those few cards between the keys. When you turn around and have them move their card to another part of the deck, you're really getting

them to reveal which of those few cards is their selected card!

Simply compare your (very short) memorized list to what you

see in front of you, and by noticing which card is missing, you'll

instantly know their card!

 VIDEO DEMO

bit.ly/1DtO75C

THE CARD TRICK YOU CAN'T SCREW UP!

IMPRESSIVENESS: 4/5

★ ★ ★ ★ ☆

CLASS: TWEENER

FACTORS: SUPER SIMPLE, IMPRESSES YOURSELF

REQUIRES: CARDS

This trick really does feel like magic. I don't understand it, and more importantly, I don't need to. All I know is that I follow all the steps, and then there's this awesome moment when the cards appear to speak directly to me, revealing the last hidden card.

To Begin: Grab a deck and thoroughly shuffle the cards. Hold the deck face-up in dealing position and deal the first card onto the table. Starting with the number value of the first card dealt, continue to deal cards on this pile as you count upwards until you reach the number 13.

In Other Words: If the first card dealt into the pile was 9, you would continue to deal cards on top, counting "ten, eleven, twelve, thirteen," for a total of five cards in the pile. If your first card

dealt was a queen (a value of twelve), you would deal only one more card onto the pile (because 12 + 1 = 13). If you dealt a six, you would deal and count "seven, eight, nine, ten, eleven, twelve, thirteen," on top, giving you eight cards in the pile. Remember that aces count as 1, jacks are 11, queens are 12, and kings are 13 (kings would, therefore, be a complete pile as soon as they're dealt).

Each time you finish a pile, move on to start another one. Keep going until you have a bunch of piles and end when you don't have enough cards left in your hand to make a complete pile (keeping these last few cards in your hand).

To Amaze Yourself: Pick any three piles at random and turn them face-down. Scoop up all the other cards and add them to the cards in your hand. Of the three face-down piles, choose any two of them and turn over the top card in each. Now that you have two face-up cards and one face-down pile, you're going to "ask" the cards to tell you the value of that final face-down card.

Start by dealing ten face-down cards from you hand onto the table. Next, deal down the numeric value of the first face-up card you selected. Last, deal down a number of cards equal to the value of the second faceup card.

Here's the magic part: count out the number of cards remaining in your hand ... that number will predict the value of the top card of the last face-down pile.

VIDEO DEMO

bit.ly/1Gd03jb

You can perform it for yourself or try it with a friend, but this one really has to be performed to be appreciated. So grab a deck and go for it!

THE AMAZING iCARD

AUDIO COMMENTARY

bit.ly/1DtOaOZ

EPISODE

bit.ly/1IaUvX7

IMPRESSIVENESS: 5/5

★ ★ ★ ★ ★

CLASS: OPENER

FACTORS: SUPER SIMPLE, IMPRESSES YOURSELF

REQUIRES: SMARTPHONE, INCLUDED GRAPHICS

I love Daniel Garcia. He's brilliant, funny, and talented, and (best of all) was kind enough to share one my favorite tricks from the Daniel Garcia Project on Scam School. You'll need to do a little preparation for this one, but once you're set, you'll have a stunner that you can perform any time, anywhere.

Setting Up: These directions are for performing the trick with an iPhone, but I'm sure you can adapt them to other smartphones as well. Start by placing all of the images attached in this chapter into a folder on your iPhone. Then fold up a two of hearts, rest it in your fingertips, set your iPhone on top, and you're set.

What They See: Explain to your friend that they're going to pick a card from the mish-mash of cards displayed on your phone. "But don't pick an obvious card like an ace," you say. "Everyone always picks an ace. Oh, and make sure you see both the number and the suit."

DOWNLOAD THE SLIDESHOW FILES HERE

bit.ly/1bGtXPC

Glancing around, they eventually mentally select the two of hearts. "Got one?" you ask. "Excellent. Now watch as all the cards vanish, and we're left with just one folded-up card." True to form, the mashup of card has cross-faded into the image of a single, folded-up playing card. "Which card are you thinking of?" you ask, and they reply that they're thinking of the two of hearts.

Now this is the part that will blow their mind: you reach forward with your right hand to pinch the image of the card, and then, with a swiping motion, you visibly pull the image of the card out from the phone, transforming it into a physical card.

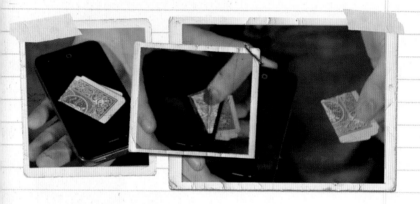

As if that's not enough, when the card is unfolded they're stunned to see it's their thought-of card, the two of hearts.

The Work: Most of this trick does itself. First, you'll just need to set up a folder of images on your iPhone as detailed below. Next, fold up a two of diamonds to match the force card, and place it in your left hand, just beneath the iPhone.

To begin the trick, press "play" at the bottom of the first image to start a slideshow. The first images displayed are a true mashup of several random playing cards, including sixes, sevens, and several other cards. This is the image you show to everyone except your volunteer, as you wait for the slideshow to advance to your force-card image. With a little timing, you can remove the phone from everyone's view right as the slideshow changes the image from the "fair" mashup of cards to the "force" mashup.

This second image contains nothing but various aces and several twos of hearts. Since you ask them not to choose an ace, you're guaranteed they can only mentally select a two of hearts. (Remind them that they need to see both the number and suit to choose a card.)

Again, with practice you'll get the timing down to draw their attention to the phone just as the slideshow cross-fades to the image of the single card. As soon as this card shows up, touch and slightly move the image to give the impression that it's a physical object trapped inside the phone. This is doubly important because this action will also stop the slideshow and allow you to pull off

your finale: with your right hand, reach up to pinch the phone, with your thumb on top of the image of the card and your middle fingers underneath the phone, pinching the actual card you've been covering up there up against the phone.

Keep pinching the screen and the card as you pull your hand to the right, swiping your fingers across the phone. Since the image will advance with your motion, you'll see an amazing visual transformation as the image of the card leaves the screen exactly as the physical card emerges from behind the phone. It really does look like you've just plucked the card out of the phone! It's really impressive and a total surprise.

Finally, wrap things up by revealing that the card matches their selection, and accept your well-deserved applause. I can't say

enough about what a fooler this is. If you ever see him, make sure
to hit up Daniel Garcia and tell him thanks for sharing this treat
with us.

VIDEO DEMO

bit.ly/1HM7Un5

The Amazing SCORCHED CARD

AUDIO COMMENTARY

bit.ly/1JZzOeA

EPISODE

bit.ly/1Pir7Nx

IMPRESSIVENESS: 3/5

★ ★ ★ ☆ ☆

CLASS: TWEENER

FACTORS: HINDU SHUFFLE, SIMPLE MECHANICS

REQUIRES: DECK OF CARDS, CANDLE

This is another gem Daniel was kind enough to share with us: it's got a fantastic pain-to-glory ratio and (best of all) uses skills you already learned in the Vanishing Card Trick chapter.

How it Looks: The cards are freely shuffled, and a card is selected and signed. The signed card is lost in the pack, and the deck is replaced into its box. Finally, the box is set on top of a cocktail candle, where it chokes off the air supply and kills the candle's flame.

However, as soon as the deck is removed from the candle, the flame returns. The cards are removed from the box and spread out face-down on the table, where one card now has a large, black

scorch mark on the back of the card. When flipped over, everyone is amazed to see it's their signed card.

The Work: Before this trick begins, you'll need to prepare one card with a scorch mark. You don't need to actually burn the card (since that will warp it and be detectible on the face-side), but instead move it around quickly over a candle flame or lighter. You'll get more soot this way and keep the card in good shape.

Once you've prepared your scorched card, place it on the bottom of the deck and you're ready to begin.

For the first part of this trick, we're going to use the same Hindu shuffle force that you just learned in The Vanishing Card trick. Shuffle through the cards, and remember to make a big deal about how fair you're being. Remind them that they really can say "stop" any time they want (not that it'll change the card they get).

Once they say "stop," show them the bottom-most card in your right hand, as you turn over the cards in your left hand. Replace the cards from your right hand face-up onto the pack in your left hand. (This way you'll be able to set their selection on the table without them seeing the scorched back of the card.) Have them sign their name across the face of the card, replace it back in the pack, and just like that: hard work is finished.

From here on out, it's all just play-acting. Place the deck on the candle, but keep a small crack for air in there. The flame will get very, very low but still burn as you talk about the flames "looking" for the card or other such nonsense. When you spread the cards out and "discover" the scorched card, remember to preserve that moment of anticipation as long as you can before flipping the card over . . . this is a miracle, and you need to remind them of that.

GET A BEER FOR A DOLLAR

AUDIO COMMENTARY

bit.ly/1JZzOLC

EPISODE

bit.ly/1KH9s1a

IMPRESSIVENESS: 4/5

★ ★ ★ ★ ☆

CLASS: TWEENER

FACTORS: NO SLEIGHT OF HAND, IMPRESSIVE RESULTS

REQUIRES: DOLLAR BILL, DECK OF CARDS

This one's another genius treat from Daniel Garcia. Have I already mentioned that you should buy everything he's ever created?

I did, didn't I . . .

The Trick: Pull out a dollar bill, set it face down on the table, and announce: "I'm about to try a challenge, and if I fail, I'll give you this dollar bill and buy beers for everyone at the table. Sound good?"

Split the deck into multiple sections and hand each section to a different person. "Everybody shuffle up some cards. I want everyone to participate, so you know there's no way I could be controlling the order of the cards." After the cards are thoroughly shuffled, have the cards reassembled into a full deck and ask one of your friends to deal 10 cards into your hands.

Looking at your cards, ask them to pick up the dollar bill and take a look at the serial number. "Here's my challenge. I'm going to try to match the cards you dealt me to as many digits as possible from that serial number. What's the first digit?"

They announce it's a 9. "Cool! I've got a nine," you say.

The next digit is a 4. "Got one of those, too."

As they read out the remaining digits of 5, 2, 7, 7, 9, and 4, you lay down cards matching every single one of them.

But you're left with two cards. "Wait. Is that all of them?" you ask. "What about letters?" and sure enough, there's a "K" that exactly matches your king, and an "A" that matches your Ace!

The Work: Before you can perform this trick, you'll need to track down a dollar bill with letters next to the serial number that can be matched from a deck of cards. Once you find a bill with K's, A's, Q's, or J's on them, you're set.

The method behind this trick is supremely simple: before you begin, just set up the top 10 cards of the deck to exactly match the serial number (you might need to get creative to exactly match the digits on the bill. Use an Ace to match "1," and a 10 or joker to match "0").

At the very beginning of the trick (when you hand out the deck in pieces to be shuffled), give out your 10-card stack as the first block of cards. Obviously, no amount of shuffling will change the contents of the stack, so when they re-assemble the cards, just make sure your 10-cards stack ends up back on top.

The rest works itself: they deal you the top 10 cards (your prepared stack), and you take credit for a minor miracle.

UNBEATABLE

NumberPuzzles

AUDIO COMMENTARY

bit.ly/1aLb4u4

EPISODE

bit.ly/1DPse08

IMPRESSIVENESS: 4/5 - 5/5

★ ★ ★ ★ ★

CLASS: CLOSERS

FACTORS: AGONIZINGLY CLEVER PUZZLES

REQUIRES: PEN AND PAPER

Stop. Stop reading forward. Stop and pay attention to me here: If I were you, I'd hit this chapter and think:

"Number puzzles? Oh, great . . . MATH. I'm sure that'll go over great at the bar . . . Pfft . . . Man, Brushwood, you've changed. You used to be all punk rock and crazy stunts, getting me drunk at the bar for free . . . Now you're pushing math on me?? I don't even know you anymore."

First off, that was very rude of you to think. I invite you into my book, and this is how you repay me? I think you owe me an apology.

Second, let me make this clear: these may be the very best, most satisfying puzzles in all of Scam School history. They don't really have anything to do with math. Each one completely fooled me, and the actual answers are incredibly satisfying.

So let's have a challenge, shall we? I'll lay out all three puzzles, and you'll promise to only look at the answers after you've given up and admit that they've outsmarted you. Deal?

Challenge the First! Check out this equation: 5+5+5=550

$$5+5+5=550$$

Your challenge is to add exactly one line and make the equation true. (Again, I said "make the equation true," which means you can't just draw a slash through the equal sign.)

I'm serious here. Don't keep reading until either you think you've solved it, or been utterly crushed under the weight of the mental strain.

Give up? Maybe you'll have more luck with . . .

Challenge the Second! Use one number exactly 3 times to add up to 60, you can only use the addition function (+), and the solution CANNOT be 20+20+20=60.

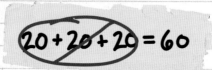

Sounds impossible, right? Same rules. Don't keep reading until you're willing to buy me a beer for the answer.

And finally . . .

Challenge the Third! Make a true equation using each of the following numbers and symbols once, and only once: 2, 3, 4, 5, +, and =

Assignments are due at the end of class. Please show your work.

The Solutions:

Are you cheating? Be honest. Because this is your last chance to personally feel the same frustrations that your targets will feel at the bar. If you're truly at your wit's end, here are the solutions . . .

Challenge the First:

$$5 + 5 + 5 = 550$$

To make the equation true, simply add one line to the first (or second) plus, and convert the equation to 545 + 5 = 550.

$$545 + 5 = 550$$

Challenge the Second:

Using the same number three times, simply write out 5 + 55 = 60.

$$5 + 55 = 60$$

Challenge the Third:

Using all the provided numbers and symols exactly once, you can get:

$$4 + 5 = 3^2$$

Many thanks to Michael Barlow, Joe Mattigan, and Jeffrey Cohen for sending me these brain-busters! I can't express how many times some of our very best episodes come straight from the viewers.

BALANCED NAILS

IMPRESSIVENESS: 3/5

★ ★ ★ ☆ ☆

CLASS: CLOSER

FACTORS: USES UNCOMMON OBJECTS AT BARS

REQUIRES: LOTS OF NAILS

AUDIO COMMENTARY

bit.ly/1blevc1

EPISODE

bit.ly/1KH9ztL

This puzzle totally stumped me the first time I saw it. The nature of the props means you probably won't perform this at the bar, but the next time you're working on any construction project you'll definitely be able to stump your friends.

The Challenge: Grab 10 to 13 nails. Hammer one nail into any surface (in a pinch, you can just have someone hold it in their hands) and challenge your mark to balance ALL the remaining nails on just the head of the first nail.

They'll think you're crazy, but assure them it can be done and without any other external apparatus of any kind.

The Solution: Once they give up (and of course, buy you a drink for the answer), lay down one of the nails flat on the table and begin setting the remaining nails side-by-side pointing in opposite directions, with the heads-side of each nail resting on the first laid-flat nail. Finally, set the very last nail on top of the first nail, facing the opposite direction. You should now have a bizarre "nail sandwich."

Hold the edges of your top and bottom nails and slowly pick the structure up. As it lifts, the heads of all the nails will hook onto the top nail, changing your nail-sandwich into a freestanding "house of nails."

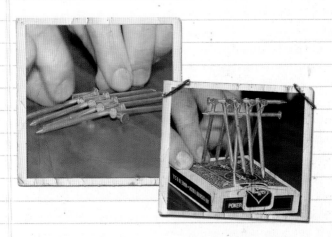

The best part is that the new structure of these nails lowers
the center of gravity so far that it becomes simple to balance all 10
to 12 nails on the head of the very first nail. Just place the structure
on the original, planted nail, and you've earned yourself a free cold
one . . . Congrats!

VIDEO DEMO

bit.ly/1bdK2fm

3 Caps 1 BEER

AUDIO COMMENTARY

bit.ly/1IxMGYd

EPISODE

bit.ly/1Eaa369

IMPRESSIVENESS: 3/5

★ ★ ★ ☆ ☆

CLASS: CLOSER

FACTORS: SIMPLE SETUP, SATISFYING PAYOFF

REQUIRES: 3 COINS OR BOTTLE CAPS

This one's a simple puzzle with an impossible-sounding setup. Just remember that the key is to keep your rules for the challenge as simple and as intuitive as possible. Grab 3 coins or 3 bottle caps, and set up this task:

The Rules:

- **Cap #1 (the face-down cap on the left):** You can touch, move, prod, and play with. There are no restrictions on this one, except you can't pick it up (don't worry: you won't need to pick it up to solve the puzzle).

- **Cap #2 (the right-side up cap in the middle):** Pretend this guy is totally rooted to the ground. You can touch it and poke it all you want, but it can't move anywhere.

- **Cap #3 (the face-down cap on the right):** This guy's tricky. Imagine he's radioactive and some kind of antimatter version of Cap #1. You can't touch him, and (worse yet) if Cap #1 touches him, it'll cause an antimatter explosion and the world will end.

The Challenge: Within those rules, start with the caps in a row of #1- #2-#3, and end with them in the order of #2-#1-#3. In other words, within the above restrictions, get the first cap between the other two.

The Solution: Since you can touch #2, place your finger firmly on top of it. Then use your other finger to slide #1 around and use it to briskly hit #2. Cap #2 won't move, but the force of the blow will pass through the bottle cap, sending cap #3 sliding off to the side. Once this is done, simply move #1 into the new gap, and collect yourself a free drink.

I know some people will insist that Cap #2 must be moving in this solution, but trust me: it's not. Just Google "Newton's Cradle" to learn more. From Wikipedia:

> The impact produces a shock wave that propagates through the intermediate balls. Any efficiently elastic material such as steel will do this as long as the kinetic energy is temporarily stored as potential energy in the compression of the material rather than being lost as heat.

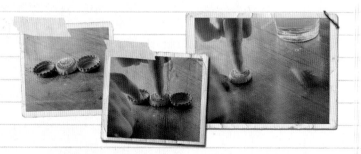

VIDEO DEMO

bit.ly/1bleB3s

Straw Puzzle Teepee

AUDIO COMMENTARY

bit.ly/1bdK4nt

EPISODE

bit.ly/1OUjAJV

IMPRESSIVENESS: 4/5

★ ★ ★ ★ ☆

CLASS: CLOSER

FACTORS: LARGER SETUP, SOLID CHALLENGE

REQUIRES: NAPKINS, STRAWS

I first saw this puzzle at the Electric Lounge in Austin, Texas. I've always loved it, and I've never had anyone figure it out.

The Setup: Grab 3 straws and cut (or tear) one of them in half. Take one of the full-length straws and fold it in half, placing a crease in the fold so it stays in a "V" shape. On a cocktail napkin, make a lean-to using the "V" and the small half-length piece you cut off. (If you have a hard time balancing the "V" on the half-length straw, try adding a notched ending for it to rest on.)

Once assembled, they should look somewhat like a pyramid or tetrahedron.

The Challenge: Pick up both straws off the first napkin and set them down on another napkin using only a full-length straw. Your tool-straw can't be folded over or made into pincers. You can't touch anything but the tool-straw with your hands, and you have to pick up both straws at once.

The Solution: Insert your tool-straw under the pinnacle of your leanto. If you push outwards on the folded-over straw, the short straw will fall down onto your tool-straw.

Now slowly pull your tool upwards, and the short straw will lock into the "V" straw.

. . . Now just lift, and you've done it!

VIDEO DEMO

bit.ly/1OyHOyV

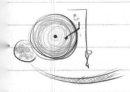

the HEIST

AUDIO COMMENTARY

bit.ly/1H8uCqr

EPISODE

bit.ly/1AA5LEE

IMPRESSIVENESS: 3/5

★★★☆☆

CLASS: CLOSER

FACTORS: COUNTER INTUITIVE SOLUTION

REQUIRES: 2 PINT GLASSES, WOODEN MATCHES, $20 BILL

I love this one. And I love "the heist" as a plot device . . . it sets you up to overact and makes the challenge feel less like a tedious puzzle and more like a grand adventure. All you need is a match, two pint glasses and a "treasure" and you'll be drinking free all night!

The Setup: Turn an empty pint glass upside down and place a "treasure" inside (in this case, a $20 bill). Set another empty pint glass upside down next to it. Finally, set up the "alarm system": a match, suspended between the two pints.

The Challenge: Liberate Andrew Jackson from his pint-glass prison, without setting off the "alarm system." You can use anything on the table, but you must adhere to the rules:

1. You can't touch the match.
2. You can only touch one of the two glasses.
3. The moment the match loses contact with the pint glass holding the money, the alarm goes off, the police attack, and you lose.

Can you do it?

The Solution: Use another match to light the head of the "alarm system" match. Just after it flares up, blow it out. You'll find the match is now tenuously fused to the pint glass. With a steady hand, you'll be able to lift the pint glass, taking the match along with it.

Now just remove the bill, replace the glass . . . and order yourself a free beer!

VIDEO DEMO

bit.ly/1zCA9xI

the HEIST

AUDIO COMMENTARY

bit.ly/1bleKUs

EPISODE

bit.ly/1FKSOcn

IMPRESSIVENESS: 4/5

★ ★ ★ ★ ☆

CLASS: CLOSER

FACTORS: ENVIRONMENTAL CONDITIONS AFFECT OUTCOME

REQUIRES: NICKEL, WOODEN MATCH, CLEAR GLASS OR CUP, STRAW OR COMB

A second heist! Every bit as harrowing and exciting as the first. I especially love that you can use the exact same theme for two tricks in a row but have a completely different setup and unique solution.

The Setup: Balance a nickel (the treasure of the ancients!) on its side on the table. Balance a wooden matchstick on top of the nickel. Finally, cover the whole arrangement with a plastic cup or pint glass (whichever you discover works best for you).

The Challenge: So the nickel is the prize. The cup? That's the fortress. See that match? It's your security alarm, and as long as the match is balanced on the nickel, it's completely active, and fully wired to the fortress. As long as the security system is active, anything touching, shaking, or moving the cup will activate the alarm. Your job: disable the alarm system WITHOUT setting off the alarm!

The first thing they're going to want to try is to hit the table. Remind them that there are seismic sensors, and if it's shaking the match, it's shaking the cup, too! In fact, be aggressive, here: anytime they get anywhere near the cup, loudly remind them of all the rules: Nothing can touch, move or vibrate the fortress while the alarm is active.

The Solution: This one sounds impossible (and it almost is). No amount of blowing, shaking, tapping or physical manipulation will get the match off without setting off the alarm.

However, if you use static electricity to charge a straw (as we did in the "Science Friction" chapter of the first *Scam School* book), you can use the static attraction to pull the match off the nickel without setting off the alarm!

If you haven't picked up Book 1 yet (and shame on you if that's the case . . . it's a delightful book!), here's what we explained: simply pinch down tightly on the straw wrapper as you slide it off of the straw, and you'll instantly charge it . . . there's no need to rub the straw on anything. Of course, if you need more charge, then rub away.

> **NOTE:** Every area has different attributes for static electricity. Sometimes the static charge will affect objects 5-6 inches away, other times only 2-3 inches. Depending on the humidity in the air, you may need to choose between a glass or plastic tumbler to act as your fortress. Make sure to practice this one with the exact materials you plan to use in your performance before attempting it on a friend.

VIDEO DEMO

bit.ly/1Gb4KXX

The HEIST 3

AUDIO COMMENTARY

bit.ly/1yLjahQ

EPISODE

bit.ly/1K8oWut

Yet another setup for a heist!

The Prison: This time there's no fortress, but instead two guards support the alarm system. Grab a box of wooden matches and place two of them in opposite corners of the slightly-opened tray, leaning them against each other as shown. First, set the treasure on the box. (If you're going to use a bill, I'd recommend weighing it down with a coin.) Next, set the alarm system by balancing a third matchstick so that one end rests on the coin and the other end leans on the heads of the guard-matches

The Rules: Your job (naturally) is to steal the treasure, but you can't directly touch any of the matches. They can move and be

moved, but as soon as the alarm system loses contact with the guards, you're busted.

When setting up this challenge, it's important to choose your words carefully to encourage them to think in terms of manipulating the matches without directly touching them. They're so precariously balanced, no amount of careful handling will prevent the alarm match from falling off if it's moved . It'll (hopefully) drive them nuts.

The Solution: This one's fun to watch. Grab a match from a different box and use it to light all three match heads on fire. (Most people won't try this, since your intuition would suggest that the burning matches would just fall apart and set off the alarm.)

Instead, the matches will start burning at the top and remain connected to each other as the flames work their way down. Once they get halfway down, however, something amazing happens: the alarm match will curl and rise up off the treasure completely on its own, as if it's begging you to take it!

Even when people think there's something to the idea of setting the matches on fire, they certainly won't expect this. (Speaking of which, I wouldn't set up this challenge for anyone who has already seen The Heist #1, since the solution is so similar.)

AIRLIFT ESCAPE

AUDIO COMMENTARY

bit.ly/1Gb5NXZ

IMPRESSIVENESS: 3/5

★ ★ ★ ☆ ☆

CLASS: PUZZLE CHALLENGE

FACTORS: REQUIRES CAREFUL VERBAL SETUP FOR MAXIMUM IMPACT

REQUIRES: SALT, PEPPER,

This puzzle has a really cool payoff, but it needs the right setup for proper impact. It's not the kind of challenge that has just one solution, but the solution you do reveal will clearly be the most elegant and satisfying. As a result, you'll have to tell a fun, compelling narrative leading up to your solution.

The Setup: Grab some salt and pepper, and you'll need some rice, too. (The salt shakers at bars usually have rice mixed in with the salt to keep the salt loose and dry.) If there's no rice available, you'll have to find a stand-in: something granular that's about as big as rice grains (maybe some gravel from the parking lot?).

Pour a small pile of rice and salt on the table, then add pepper liberally. Flatten out the pile and spread them around so it looks like this photo.

The Scene: Prison. These poor grains of salt and pepper are prisoners of war. The grains of rice? They're the guards, and they're very, very sensitive. In fact, anything moving them even just the slightest bit will raise the alarm.

The Challenge: Get as many grains of salt and pepper out of that prison, as fast as you can, but without disturbing the rice-guards.

Most people will begin by trying to blow on the salt, which will immediately send the rice rolling and raise the alarm. You could poke around at the fringes with your fingers, looking for salt and pepper grains that are far enough from the rice that you can snatch them away to safety . . . but that's going to take a long time and is of no help to the poor souls deeper inside the camp.

The Solution: There will be a lot of solutions proposed by your friends, but I don't think any will be as effective (or elegant)

as this one: Grab a paper-wrapped straw from the bar and pinch it tightly as you pull off the wrapper. This will charge the straw with static electricity, just as we learned in Scam School Book 1 for the effect "Science Friction" and again in this book for "The Heist 2."

With a charged straw, you'll be able to swoop in like an airship, and the static electricity will cause the salt and pepper to leap up from the table and attach themselves to the straw. The rice will be too heavy to be lifted, and those guards will have no idea their prisoners are being snatched away in the dead of night!

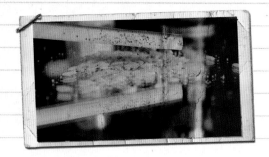

We experimented with a lot of different combinations and discovered that adding pepper vastly increased the salt's responsiveness to the static charge. For an ideal setup, you can use just pepper and rice (though that seems a little more tricky to me).

VIDEO DEMO

bit.ly/1JmIWcg

IMPRESSIVENESS: 3/5

★ ★ ★ ☆ ☆

CLASS: OPENER

FACTORS: FRUSTRATING CHALLENGE

REQUIRES: PACK OF CIGARETTES

The CIGARETTE~ STUMP

AUDIO COMMENTARY

bit.ly/1GOCoxa

EPISODE

bit.ly/1bsmnrl

Here's a super short-and-sweet puzzle that'll stump any smoker.

The Setup: Grab their pack of cigarettes and pull the cellophane halfway off the cigarette box. Use a lit cigarette to melt a hole right in the center.

Next, tear off just the filter of another cigarette and drop it inside the hole. (Make sure you remove every little bit of extra paper at the top . . . you can burn it away if you want to be super-thorough.) Once dropped inside, the filter should rattle around freely.

The Challenge: You can touch the box, but you can't manipulate the cellophane that hangs off of it. Your job is to get that filter out of the cellophane prison, right through the hole.

People will immediately start shaking the box, but no matter how long you shake it about, you'll never get the filter out that way.

The Solution: This works a little easier with soft-sided boxes, but if you put a little bend in the box itself, you can blow down the side of the box and directly into the cellophane chamber. The filter will dance all around the chamber, eventually flying right out!

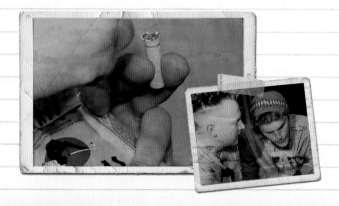

This is one you'll really want to practice beforehand. Tiny differences in the size of the hole and filter will make a huge difference. For best success, keep the filter small, and position the hole toward the ground when you blow.

VIDEO DEMO

bit.ly/1zCB7tN

PUZZLES FOR HOT CHICKS

AUDIO COMMENTARY

bit.ly/1IxOKj2

EPISODE

bit.ly/1KH9W7B

IMPRESSIVENESS: 2/5

★ ★ ★ ☆ ☆

CLASS: TWEENERS

FACTORS: CONVERSATION STARTERS, EASY SOLUTIONS

REQUIRES: MATCHES OR TOOTHPICKS

Sometimes the best way to win is to lose. After all: if you're the jerk who always wins every challenge at the bar, pretty soon you'll have nobody to play with. For those times when the goal isn't to score free drinks, here are a few never-fail ways to get the hottest girls at the bar to talk with you for at least 20 minutes.

. . . You might just end up losing the challenges, but winning some phone numbers.

The Setup: So you know a ton of unbeatable puzzles, but now it's important you learn a few beatable puzzles. Maybe you just want to soften your mark up for the kill. Or maybe you've spotted a hottie that you'd like to make feel smart. Whatever your reason, here are three medium-difficulty match puzzles that are just as likely to be solved as they are to stump your mark:

#1 - The Puppy Dog: This one's perfect for the girls. It's cute, cartoony, adorable, and most importantly . . . solvable. Set up the doggie as pictured. This is the puppy before he got run over.

Moving two matches, show the puppy as he looks AFTER he got run over.

#2 - The Fishy: Another cute animal puzzle. Set up the fish as pictured, then ask this question: Moving only three matches, can you make the fish swim the exact opposite direction?

#3 - The Giraffe: This one surprises me . . . I thought it'd be simple, but experience has shown me that it's a reasonably difficult stumper.

Set up the giraffe as pictured, then ask: moving only one match, can you change the orientation of the giraffe?

(Note the difference in verbiage here. On the fish, we said he has to be swimming "the exact opposite direction." In this case, we just want the giraffe to be facing any other direction).

Don't forget: you're in charge here. If a jealous boyfriend butts in, or if the girls start giving you too much sass, hit 'em up with the teepee puzzle or the four quarters trick from Book 1. If they really start bugging you, remember there's always the coin on the forehead trick.

The Solutions:

#1- The Puppy Dog: Just move the two inner legs to the other side of the body, and you've got a cartoon-style, flattened pooch.

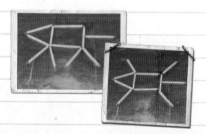

 VIDEO DEMO #1

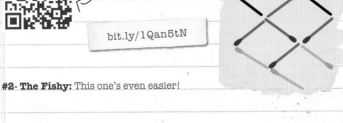

bit.ly/1Qan5tN

#2- The Fishy: This one's even easier!

VIDEO DEMO #2

bit.ly/1E2kBbM

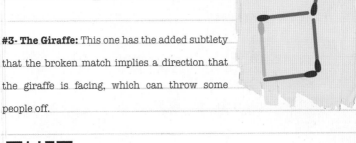

#3- The Giraffe: This one has the added subtlety that the broken match implies a direction that the giraffe is facing, which can throw some people off.

 VIDEO DEMO #3

bit.ly/1F7wgHe

OVER THE WALL

AUDIO COMMENTARY

bit.ly/1Ho86Zk

EPISODE

bit.ly/1GVF7xE

IMPRESSIVENESS: 3/5

★ ★ ★ ☆ ☆

CLASS: CLOSER

FACTORS: SIMPLE CHALLENGE

REQUIRES: EMPTY BEER BOTTLE, STRAW, "WALL" TO SCALE

I had seen parts of this trick before, but always with an unsatisfying opening: "pick up this bottle using this one straw!" The setup was just too perfect, too impossible. It begged people to think unconventionally, and once they did, most of the folks I tried it on were able to noodle out the solution.

So for Scam School, we worked on changing the setup to create a compelling challenge that would encourage people to think in more straightforward terms, so the ending would be a nice slap in the face. The first thing we did was change the goal: it's not just to "pick up this bottle," but to, without touching the bottle with your hands, pick it up off the table, get it over a wall of condiments, and safely land it on the other side. Oh, and the only tool you're allowed to use are these two straws . . . here's what it looked like:

The Setup: Grab two straws and an empty beer bottle. On the straws, use a pen, marker, or scratch marks to mark a "no man's land" of about 2- 3 inches in the center of each straw.

The Rules: Neither you nor the bottle is allowed to touch anything in this "no man's land" area on either straw. Each independent side of each straw can touch either you (your fingers) or the beer bottle, but no one side of a straw can touch both you and the bottle at the same time.

The Challenge: Staying within these rules, use the straws to pick up the bottle off the table, carry it over the wall, and land it safely on the other side.

The Solution: The abundance of
rules and tools virtually guarantees that
they'll miss the actual method. Usually
they'll start by trying to use the straws as
chopsticks, but discover that they're useless
without touching the no-mans-land. Next
they might hold the bottom of each straw
and attempt to push up on the lip of the
bottle, but find it impossible to balance.

After they've made a mess of their attempts (and once they
promise you a beer for the answer), reveal the truth: you only need
one of the two straws.

If you crease a "hook" into one of the sides and slowly and
carefully slide it down the neck of the bottle, it will hit a "sweet
spot" where it's wedged in the neck of the bottle. Once that happens,
it's a snap to pull it up and over the wall. To release, just dip the
straw back down.

VIDEO DEMO

bit.ly/1zCBcO1

CAGED COPPERHEADS

AUDIO COMMENTARY

bit.ly/1D60Hrc

EPISODE

bit.ly/1JM5Ddv

IMPRESSIVENESS: 3/5

★ ★ ★ ☆ ☆

CLASS: CLOSER

FACTORS: LARGER SETUP

REQUIRES: 9 PENNIES, PAPER AND PEN

This one's pretty simple. You can do it with just a pen and paper, but then every wrong attempt will require you to start again and redraw the entire setup. When we tried this on Scam School, we used physical pennies and matches. It's a sloppier configuration, but it's easier to move stuff around while they experiment.

The Scene: Draw 9 dots in a 3x3 grid, surrounded by a box. Alternately, you can lay out 9 pennies in a grid on the table, surrounding them by a square fence of matchsticks.

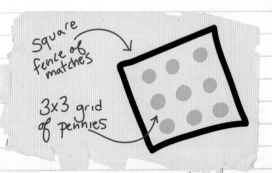

Square fence of matches

3x3 grid of pennies

Those pennies? They're copperheads. Dangerous snakes that you're charged with separating from each other. However your farmer boss is a cheap jerk and says you may only build two square-shaped fences to accomplish the task.

Your Challenge: Drawing or building only 2 squares, get each dot/penny/rattlesnake in its own, completely separate cage. No two copperheads can reach each other or they'll fight and you'll lose your job!

The Solution: Nobody said the cages had to be consistent in size or shape with each other . . . so inscribe the whole pen with one large, diagonal square and then inscribe another square within the diagonal one.

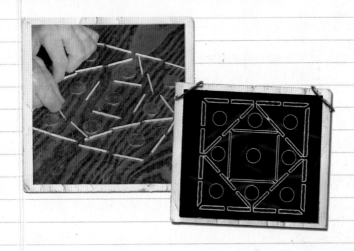

And there you have it: nine safely separated, dangerous, pissed-off snakes.

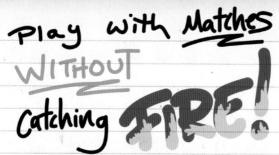

Play with Matches
WITHOUT
Catching FIRE!

AUDIO COMMENTARY

bit.ly/1aLcUuJ

EPISODE

bit.ly/1ztOrro

I like coupling these two matchstick puzzles together, since each requires you to approach the problem from a completely different mindset. Often times the very act of switching mental gears makes it harder for them to solve an otherwise simple puzzle.

Math Mashup: Set up matchsticks to make the Roman numeral expression "seven equals one," as shown here:

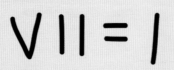

Obviously no matter how you read it, this equation is wrong . . . but by moving just one match, you can make it a true equation. (And no: it doesn't count to change the equals sign into a "does not equal" sign.)

Figure it out? Try puzzle number two:

The Grid: Start by setting up the matchsticks to create a grid of sixteen squares . . .

The Challenge: Remove just 9 matches to end up with absolutely no squares. Obviously you'll have rectangles, but none can have four equal sides!

The Solutions:

Math Mashup: Move one of the matches from the VII to change the equation to "the square root of one equals one."

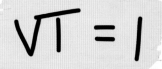

$$\sqrt{1} = 1$$

The Grid: You'll have to memorize this pattern, but once you've got it down, you'll be set!

Break down the 16 squates into 3 sections:

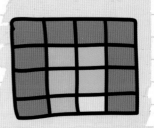

- A U-shaped run of 2-by-1 rectangles (shown here in red)
- An inner 3-by-1 rectangle (orange)
- An inner 2-by-1 rectangle, next to a missing edge (green)

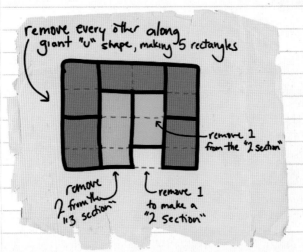

remove every other along giant "u" shape, making 5 rectangles

remove 1 from the "2 section"

remove 2 from the "3 section"

remove 1 to make a "2 section"

NAPKIN ORIGAMI PUZZLES

AUDIO COMMENTARY

bit.ly/1GOCxAv

EPISODE

bit.ly/1I8UAch

IMPRESSIVENESS: 2/5

★ ★ ☆ ☆ ☆

CLASS: TWEENERS

FACTORS: COUNTER INTUITIVE, SIMPLE

REQUIRES: NAPKINS

That's right. You read that title right.

You're going to score beer. With napkins.

And origami.

And... probably some kind of hypnosis. I don't really understand it, to be honest.

Napkin Battledrome Throwdown Challenge #1: Grab a napkin and draw these numbers as you see here:

After you've drawn the numbers on the front, make sure you flip over the napkin and duplicate them exactly mirrored on the other side. (In other words, place a "1" on the other side of the 1, and "8" on the other side of the 8, etc.)

Your Task: Figure out some way to fold up the napkin, so the digits 1- 8 all appear in sequential order from top to bottom. By the time your folds are complete, you should be able to use scissors to cut off the folded edges and deal down through the numbers straight in order.

Not gonna lie. I couldn't figure this one out and still have to look up the answer every time I go to perform it.

Napkin Battledrome Throwdown Challenge #2: Grab 3 cocktail napkins. Make sure two are plain, and one has a different design or color. Lay them out as you see here and think through this question:

"If I start rolling forward from the inner most corner of the bottommost napkin, and I stop only after I've completed one full revolution through all three napkins... what will the order of the napkins be? In other words, after I complete the roll, where will the colored napkin end up?"

Will the funky-colored napkin be on top? On bottom? In the middle? Think it through and then place your bets...

The Solutions:

Challenge #1 Answer: This one is surprisingly tough, but follow these steps and you'll be good to go. Once you've completed the folds, tear or cut off the edges so you can run through the numbers like a deck of cards.

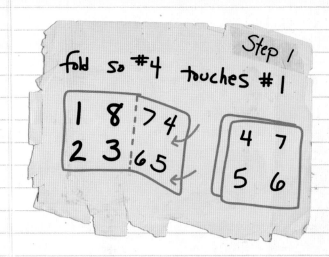

Step 1

fold so #4 touches #1

| 1 | 8 | 7 4 |
| 2 | 3 | 6 5 |

| 4 | 7 |
| 5 | 6 |

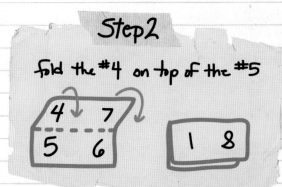

Step2

fold the #4 on top of the #5

| 4 | 7 |
| 5 | 6 |

| 1 | 8 |

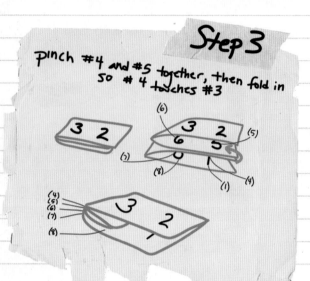

Step 3

pinch #4 and #5 together, then fold in so #4 touches #3

Step 4

fold #2 on top of #3

VIDEO DEMO #1

bit.ly/1bdLwpQ

Challenge #2 Answer: The surprising answer is that the napkin ends up in the middle. However, this is partly dependent on how tightly you roll the napkins, so be certain you practice the roll several times before you go betting a beer over it. With practice, you can even use this discrepancy to change the outcome after they place their bets.

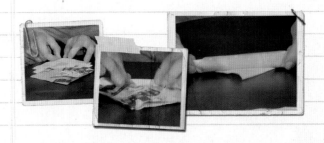

VIDEO DEMO #2

bit.ly/1D7w9a1

HARD vs IMPOSSIBLE

AUDIO COMMENTARY

bit.ly/1J2Wxc1

EPISODE

bit.ly/1ERSYmk

IMPRESSIVENESS: 4/5

★ ★ ★ ★ ☆

CLASS: CLOSER/PRANK

FACTORS: 2 PUZZLES AT ONCE

REQUIRES: PEN AND PAPER

I was completely surprised and utterly thrilled with how well this episode went. Each of the puzzles used in this challenge had been sitting in my "stuff to try" file for years, but each of them felt just a bit short of a full Scam School episode.

It was the lucky idea of combining the two that has since made this one of my all-time favorite bar challenges.

Before the Challenge: Grab some napkins and pens and let your target know that he's about to take on two separate puzzles. One of them is extremely hard . . . and the other one is impossible.

Literally impossible.

Of course, he doesn't get to know which one's hard and which one is impossible, but as long as he solves just one of them, he'll win a tasty cold beverage. Once he gives up in frustration, however, you'll let him off the hook.

Puzzle #1: Draw a collection of empty boxes in this configuration:

Their challenge is to fill the boxes with the digits 1 through 8, without ever drawing a number in a square that touches either the previous digit or the next digit (and that includes the diagonals!). Each digit must be completely separate from the digit that comes before and the digit that comes after it.

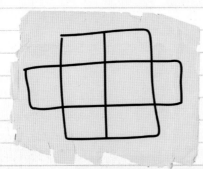

Puzzle #2: In this case, imagine you have a house with 5 rooms, as seen here:

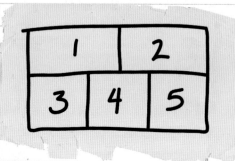

Your job, as a very bored ghost, is to discover a single path that will take you through every single wall in the building (both internal and external) exactly once.

You can cross your own path as often as you like, but if you miss a wall or go through any wall twice, you're busted.

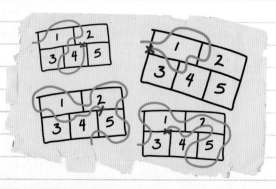

Some Thoughts: Before you find the answer on this one, I really do want you to attempt them both. If I had just hand you a single puzzle, you'll keep on trying tenaciously to solve it. Hell, you might be the type to spend hours trying it until you triumphantly emerge victorious.

But knowing that one of these puzzles is completely impossible . . . it eats at you. The entire time you're beating your head against the wall on one puzzle, you're thinking, "Man . . . what if this is a total waste? Is this the fake puzzle? Maybe I'll take another look at the other one." And before you know it, you've flipped so many times that you just want to buy a beer and be done with it.

The Solutions:

The Five-Rooms Problem: This one's a classic topology puzzle, and it's completely impossible. I've gotten dozens of emails from people convinced they've got it, only to discover they've forgotten a section of wall. Check out this Wikipedia article to learn more.

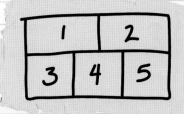

The 1 Through 8 Puzzle: This one was sent in to me by Matthew Cosme, and it annoyed the hell out of me. I knew it was just a matter of thinking it logically through, but I couldn't wrap my mind around it.

Here's the actual solution . . .

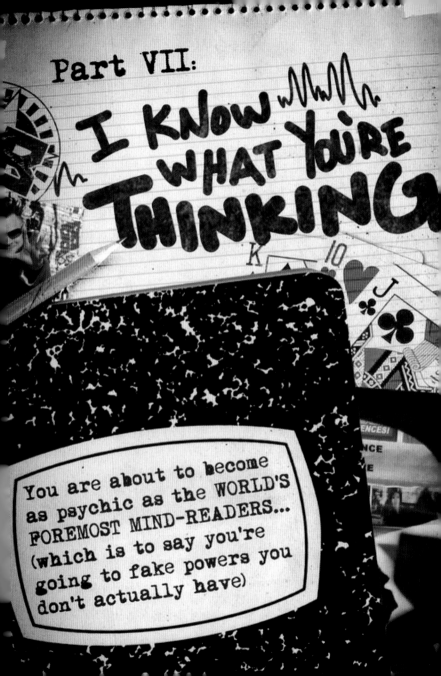

Part VII:

I KNOW WHAT YOU'RE THINKING

You are about to become as psychic as the WORLD'S FOREMOST MIND-READERS... (which is to say you're going to fake powers you don't actually have)

MIND control SCAM

IMPRESSIVENESS: 4/5

★ ★ ★ ★ ☆

CLASS: TWEENER

FACTORS: COMPLETE REMOTE EXECUTION

REQUIRES: ACCESS TO YOUTUBE

I'm not sure which is the most impressive trick we've ever taught on Scam School . . . but I do know that this one is far and away my favorite. It required over 100 video shoots, 60+ hours of editing and uploads, and can be performed literally any time, anywhere.

Oh, and plus: this trick was performed on the International Space Station.

Read that again, because it's been 4 years, and I still don't believe it.

If get my hands on a time machine, I won't change a single thing about history. But I will travel back to see 8th grader Brian Brushwood just to tell him:

"DUDE! You know Richard Garriott? Lord British? The guy who made all those Ultima video games that you love and won't stop playing? Well, in the future, he becomes so rich that he buys a trip to the International Space Station. Also: there's going to be an International Space Station.

"Anyway, by the time this happens, you're going to be an internet-famous magician who invents tricks and hosts a show called Scam School . . . and he's going to do a trick you invented in space!!

"Oh, yeah . . . you should also know there'll be this thing called 'the Internet.' And pogs. And boy bands. And eventually mustaches come back into fashion, but only ironically. I gotta go."

"WAIT! Also: buy stock in Yahoo!, but sell it before 2001!"

The Effect: Grab your friend and asks if he believes in "mind control." Not that crazy-cartoon mind-zombie stuff, but the idea that specific phrases and subtle gestures can influence what we choose.

Tell him that the only reason you ask is because you saw an interview with this crazy life-coach professor guy, and he claimed that by reciting a specific poem he could cause people to think of one specific card from a deck of cards.

"Let's try it," you say, "I'm going to read you some lines from this old Robert Frost poem, and as soon as I'm done, you're going to think of a flurry of different playing cards. After a few moments, one of them will just feel right to you. Once that happens, tell me the card you're thinking of. Ready? Here we go . . ."

> The woods are lovely, dark and deep;
>
> But I have promises to keep,
>
> And miles to go before I sleep . . .

"There . . . What card are you thinking of?"

Here's the best part: whatever card he says, you start freaking out. It's like a miracle just happened. You couldn't be more amazed if he had just turned invisible, right there before your eyes.

"SHUT. UP. Are you messing with me? You really thought of the seven of spades? Did you already see this interview?!"

When they swear that they have no idea what you're talking about, continue: "Look it up! Look it up yourself. The guy posted the interview on YouTube . . . His name is Professor Byron Doubleday."

And sure enough, after a YouTube search, he finds this interview with Professor Byron Doubleday . . .

The interview is 100% clear: Professor Byron Doubleday proclaimed years ago that once your friend heard the poem, he was destined to think of the seven of spades!

So is it real? Did the good professor really unlock "deep structures" in the human mind, allowing you to implant images?

The Work: As crazy as it sounds, I actually created 104 different versions of this interview with our mysterious expert (played by my friend and talented hypnotist, CJ Johnson), and uploaded them all under 52 different accounts on YouTube. In each interview, the expert has a different name and predicts a different card.

I know. Insane, right? I've got to give big thanks to my friend and mentalist Jonny Zavant for this one, too . . . he did a lot of the heavy lifting on the tedious edits and uploads.

The Method: When you tell the story, make sure to specifically mention the interview is with a "crazy life-coach professor guy." (This will be important when you come up with his name later.)

Only after you hear their card do you freak out and tell him to search for your expert's interview. And the name of the expert is determined by which card they chose.

Here's how you translate the card they name into the name of the expert:

Diamonds = Doctor sPades = Professor heaRts = Reverend Clubs = Coach

The Title is determined by the suit of the card selected: Diamonds = Doctor, sPades = Professor, heaRts = Reverend, and Clubs = Coach

GROUP 1
1-5
SINGLETON

GROUP 2
6-10
DOUBLEDAY

GROUP 3
11-13
TRIPLETT

His Last Name is determined by which group of numbers his card comes from: 1-5 is Singleton, 6-10 is Doubleday, and 11-13 is Triplett.

1=A=Alfred | 2=B=Byron | 3=C=Charles
4=D=David | 5=E=Edgar

His First Name is determined by which number of card it is, within its group:

1 = A = Alfred, 2 = B = Byron, 3 = C = Charles, 4 = D = David, 5 = E = Edgar

For Example: Let's take the seven of spades.

Spades means he's a "Professor."

Seven is the second number in the second group.

So we're looking for "Professor Byron Doubleday."

How about the king of hearts?

Hearts means he's a "Reverend."

King is the 3rd card in the 3rd group.

...there he is, "Reverend Charles Triplett."

You can do this trick in person, over the phone, or even over IM! If You're Just Lazy, then you're still set.

If you're reading this book on a device connected to YouTube, then just set up the trick as usual, but instead of giving the expert's name, you can just click directly on his interview from the following list at the end of this section.

Final Thoughts: There have been a few things that have changed on YouTube since this trick was first posted. For one thing, YouTube has gotten better at identifying similar videos in the column to the right of the video . . .

. . . to deal with this, just make sure to click "full screen" as soon as they find the correct video and close the video as soon as (or even before) it's finished. (Also: in the long term, you can help mask this giveaway by throwing in "Coach David Singleton" or "Reverend Alfred Triplett" as keywords and in the descriptions of random cat videos you upload. The more noise there is with these

names, the more random stuff will show up in the "related videos" off to the right.)

You can also perform the effect using any smartphone, as it

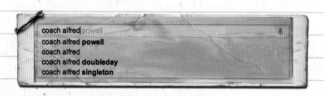

won't display the related videos while it's playing.

In the last few years, YouTube has also improved its "autocomplete" feature, so often times a YouTube search may show autocompletes that give away part of the effect.

To work around this, I do my searches on Bing or Google. The results will still take you directly to the correct video, but mask the other similar videos.

Unexpected Benefits: One of the interesting side effects of this trick is that we've been able to gather surprising information about which cards people are most likely to come up with off the top of their heads. Here's a post I wrote after the first year of the Mind Control Scam:

> Hey gang– it's been a year since we started doing the "mind control scam" YouTube card trick.
>
> One year later, and it's now been performed over 80,000 times. Since we're able to track (and log) which cards are selected

for the trick, we're inadvertently running the first large-scale survey on what cards are most likely to be thought of by a spectator in an actual performance setting.

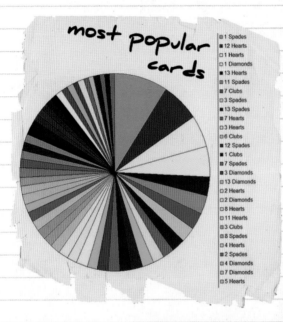

This is an interesting opportunity to find some hidden behaviors, and possibly come up with a way to exploit them, as well :-)

With a sample size of 80,000, here are the results to date (expressed first as a pie chart):

First off, surprisingly, over 25% of all hits come from only four cards: the Ace of spades, Queen of Hearts, Ace of Hearts, and Ace of Diamonds.

Only 15 cards make up 50% of the cards most likely to be thought of.

Spades was the most popular suit, with 24,000 selections.

Hearts was a close second, with almost 23,000.

Diamonds trailed at #3, with 17,300, and Clubs was a DISTANT fourth place, with 14,600 picks. (Note, this is barely more than ½ of Spades' numbers.)

The least popular card in the entire deck is the 10 of clubs.

I'd love to hear what observations you find. The full XL document is here.

In case you just want a quick glance, the raw data is given in ASCII form below (download the XL file if you plan to play with the numbers at all).

As promised, here are direct links to every interview for each individual card. Just scroll to their card, and select the link. And of course: don't let them see your work.

Diamonds:

A♦ - Doctor Alfred Singleton

2♦ - Doctor Byron Singleton

3♦ - Doctor Charles Singleton

4♦ - Doctor David Singleton

5♦ - Doctor Edgar Singleton

6♦ - Doctor Alfred Doubleday

7♦ - Doctor Byron Doubleday

8♦ - Doctor Charles Doubleday

9♦ - Doctor David Doubleday

10♦ - Doctor Edgar Doubleday

J♦ - Doctor Alfred Triplett

Q♦ - Doctor Byron Triplett

K♦ - Doctor Charles Triplett

Spades:

A♥ - Professor Alfred Singleton

2♥ - Professor Byron Singleton

3♥ - Professor Charles Singleton

4♥ - Professor David Singleton

5♥ - Professor Edgar Singleton

6♥ - Professor Alfred Doubleday

7♥ - Professor Byron Doubleday

8♥ - Professor Charles Doubleday

9♥ - Professor David Doubleday

10♥ - Professor Edgar Doubleday

J♥ - Professor Alfred Triplett

Q♥ - Professor Byron Triplett

K♥ - Professor Charles Triplett

Hearts:

A♥ - Reverend Alfred Singleton

2♥ - Reverend Byron Singleton

3♥ - Reverend Charles Singleton

4♥ - Reverend David Singleton

5♥ - Reverend Edgar Singleton

6♥ - Reverend Alfred Doubleday

7♥ - Reverend Byron Doubleday

8♥ - Reverend Charles Doubleday

9♥ - Reverend David Doubleday

10♥ - Reverend Edgar Doubleday

J♥ - Reverend Alfred Triplett

Q♥ - Reverend Byron Triplett

K♥ - Reverend Charles Triplett

Clubs:

A♣ - Coach Alfred Singleton

2♣ - Coach Byron Singleton

3♣ - Coach Charles Singleton

4♣ - Coach David Singleton

5♣ - Coach Edgar Singleton

6♣ - Coach Alfred Doubleday

7♣ - Coach Byron Doubleday

8♣ - Coach Charles Doubleday

9♣ - Coach David Doubleday

10♣ - Coach Edgar Doubleday

J♣ - Coach Alfred Triplett

Q♣ - Coach Byron Triplett

K♣ - Coach Charles Triplett

BUST 'em IN A LIE

AUDIO COMMENTARY

bit.ly/1yLkn8X

EPISODE

bit.ly/1IaWtXF

Banachek is, without exaggeration, one of the greatest mentalism thinkers in all of history. In this entire book, I don't think I could effectively list all of his contributions to the art of mind reading.

So I was unbelievably flattered when he volunteered to let us teach one of my all-time favorite tricks from his book Psychological Subtleties. This is going to start off sounding like a trick you've heard before, but trust me: it's not. This is so unbelievably fair, I honestly have trouble thinking through why it works.

How it Looks: Grab two friends. Explain that you're going to place $20 on the table and turn away. While you're turned away, have one of them steal the $20 and place it in his pocket. Don't let them tell you who the thief is!

Once you turn around, explain that you're about to have an interrogation. Just like in a real interrogation, either of them can choose to lie or tell the truth. Unlike a real-life interrogation, they must remain consistent, either always lying or always telling the truth.

This may sound like a riddle you've heard before, but remember that their decision to lie or tell the truth has nothing to do with the other guy. They can both choose to lie, or they can both choose to tell the truth, or they can be one of each . . . it doesn't matter.

The one thing you will ask them to do before you begin, however, is to lock-in their decision by whispering to the other person whether they intend to only lie, or only tell the truth. Once they're settled, remind them of how fair this setup is: Since either of them can lie or tell the truth, you have no way to know which one is doing which.

Point out that if you asked, "Are you a liar?" they'd say "no," if they were a liar, and they'd say "no," if they weren't a liar! There doesn't seem to be any way for you to know the difference, or to find out whether either of them is lying.

The Interrogation: It couldn't be simpler. Pick a person at random. "Did you steal my $20 bill?" you ask.

"No," answers your baseball-cap wearing friend.

You nod sagely, smile, then say, "Just as I thought. You just gave away everything, my friend." You turn and address your pal dressed in business-casual attire, "There's just one thing that's been itching at me: You and your buddy here, when you both made your decisions to lie or tell the truth, did you both pick the same thing?"

Smirking, he says, "yep."

"A-ha," you sigh, "which is why I know YOU have the $20 bill, Mr. Business-Casual!"

How it Works: You've got a decision to make here. You're about to learn how this works, but before you confuse yourself, decide right now if you really honestly care about why this works. I honestly think you might have more fun and get started faster if you just trust that the logic-gods have already worked it out for you . . .

Question #1: After you've performed the initial theft and setup questions, your first interrogative should be placed at a person at random. Just pick a guy, look him in the eye, and ask, "Did you take my $20 bill?"

No matter what he says here, you should remember his answer, but not yet believe it. It's the second question that tells you whether you can accept this answer at face value, or treat it as an exact lie.

Question #2: Ask the other person, "The two of you . . . when you chose to lie or tell the truth, did you both pick the exact same thing?

Q1: (first person) Did you take my bill?

Q2: (second person) Did the two of you pick the same thing?

This is the all-important answer. If he says "yes," then you know you can treat the answer to Question #1 as absolute truth. If he says "no," then treat it like a complete lie.

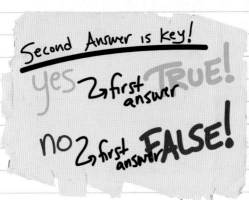

Second Answer is key!

yes → first answer TRUE!

no → first answer FALSE!

Why it Works: There's really only 3 ways this game can play out:

1. They'll both choose to tell the truth.
2. They'll both choose to lie.
3. One will lie, and one will tell the truth.

With that in mind, here's how it can go:

Situation #1: Both are truth-tellers . . . In this case, you'll ask Mr. A if he stole the $20, and he'll honestly tell you whether he did or didn't. You'll remember his answer, but then ask Mr. B, "The two of you . . . did you both pick the same thing?"

Mr. B will (truthfully) answer "yes," and then you'll know to treat Mr. A's answer as the truth (which it is).

Situation #2: Both are liars . . . In this case, you'll ask Mr. A if he stole the $20, and he'll tell you a LIE about whether he did or didn't. You'll remember his answer, but then ask Mr. B, "The two of you . . . did you both pick the same thing?"

Mr. B will (dishonestly) answer "no," and then you'll know to treat Mr. A's answer as a lie (which it is).

Situation #3: One truth-teller, one liar . . . In this case, you'll ask Mr. A if he stole the $20, and let's say he happens to be the truth-teller, so he honestly tells you whether or not he took it. You'll remember his answer, but then ask Mr. B, "Did you both pick the same thing?

Since Mr. A was the truth-teller, Mr. B is the liar, and answers "yes," unwittingly telling you that it's safe to treat Mr. A's answer as the truth (which it is). Think this through in the reverse, and you'll see it still works.

Make sure to check out Banachek's amazing back catalog of material at banachekproducts.com and drop him a note saying thanks from Scam School!

PREDICT *the* FUTURE

with DOMINOES

AUDIO COMMENTARY

bit.ly/1DtRedL

EPISODE

bit.ly/1JM65bI

IMPRESSIVENESS: 3/5

★★★☆☆

CLASS: *TWEENER*

FACTORS: SUPER EASY, YET IMPRESSIVE

REQUIRES: FULL BOX OF DOMINOES

The pain-to-glory ratio for this trick is off-the-charts. It takes nothing to set up, it's totally fair, and it's a powerful stunner prediction effect.

This effect does use a full set of dominoes, which means it's not exactly an "any time, any where" slam dunk. But if you file away this method, next time you see a set around, you can blow your friends away.

How it Looks: The mark shuffles all the dominoes, picks any domino to start, and then begins to create a long domino chain (matching ends, as they would when playing dominoes). Despite the fact that he has complete freedom of choice, you correctly predict the two numbers appearing at either side of the chain.

Why?: A surprising number of even domino players don't even know this . . . but a complete set of dominos will make a complete circle when fully played out. By removing one domino, you're predetermining where the break in the circle will come, allowing you to "predict" what numbers will be on each end! No matter what decisions they make, as long as they play out all the dominoes on the table, your prediction will be correct.

Just steal away one domino, draw its numbers on your prediction, and you're set! Easy, right?

THE MONTY HALL PARADOX

AUDIO COMMENTARY

bit.ly/1zCBpkv

EPISODE

bit.ly/1GUZ4Sn

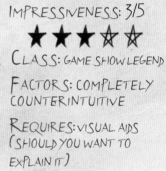

IMPRESSIVENESS: 3/5

★ ★ ★ ☆ ☆

CLASS: GAME SHOW LEGEND

FACTORS: COMPLETELY COUNTERINTUITIVE

REQUIRES: VISUAL AIDS (SHOULD YOU WANT TO EXPLAIN IT)

A while back I asked the Scam School viewers to send me their favorite, most counter-intuitive mathematics scams, and this was FAR and away the most popular one. Not only is it a curious statistical paradox, but you can use the principle to make up your own challenge using 3 cards to represent the 3 doors, with a free beer as the grand prize.

The Scene: You're on stage, playing "Let's Make a Deal" with Monty Hall. It's the 1960s, and you're rocking a very sweet lime green pinstripe suit.

Monty points to three doors on stage, explaining that behind one of them is ONE BILLION PESOS. Behind the other two doors there is only DEATH.

Wait. Not death. It's a party tray of rancid goat cheese. It just smells like death.

So you choose door #3 at random, figuring you've got a 1 in 3 chance of becoming the Warren Buffett of Tijuana, and a 2 in 3 chance of being well-equipped to host an awkward mixer for carrion-eaters.

"Now before we see what's behind door #3, let me show you what you didn't pick," Monty says. Door #1 swings wide open to reveal a lovely bikini-clad model vomiting next to a mountain of goat cheese.

With only doors #2 and #3 remaining, Monty makes you a curious offer: If you'd like, you can switch your choice from door #3 to door #2.

Should you change? Does it make any statistical difference? What would the odds be if you stayed on the same door? Take a moment and think this through before you read on.

Intuitively, most people insist that it makes no difference. They say the odds were 1 in 3 that you'd win, but now they're 1 in 2. And since there's just two doors to choose from, why would it matter if you switched? If you pick either door, it's still just one of the 2 possible doors, so your odds are 1 in 2 no matter what.

Amazingly, not only should you switch to the other door, but if you do, you're twice as likely to win. If you change doors, you actually have a 2 out of 3 chance to become rich.

The key to understanding this paradox is to remember the part when Monty opens up one of the goat cheese doors. By opening one of the goat cheese doors after you make your first selection, he reveals important information that drastically affects your chances.

Think of it this way: When you make your first choice, the odds are that you'll pick a goat cheese door. Even with the door closed, you know there's a 66% chance that you picked a loser, so you should just assume that you're currently holding a bad door.

When Monty opens the other door, he's eliminating the other loser. So if you're probably holding a loser, and the other loser has now been eliminated, you should assume that the billion pesos are behind the door you're not holding.

If you're not sure about this, try performing it on yourself or with a friend with a deck of cards, using an ace and two jokers for

your three doors. A few trials, and it'll become more intuitive for you.

Another way to think of the problem is to imagine many, many more doors.

Imagine you're playing the same game, but this time there are 10 doors. You pick door #1, and Monty opens up all the other doors except door #7. Would you switch to door #7 then?

Now imagine there's one hundred doors. You start by picking door #1, and Monty responds by revealing goat cheese behind every single door except for door #83. Would you switch then?

All of these examples reveal the same thing: you should always assume your first choice is likely goat cheese, so when all the other goat cheese doors are eliminated, the only smart move is to switch doors.

MIND-BLOWING PREDICTION GAME!

AUDIO COMMENTARY

bit.ly/1O8dZ28

EPISODE

bit.ly/1Eac8Pu

With this simple trick, you'll make spot-on predictions every time and fool your friends into thinking you're a mind-reading wizard, when really you're just a dude who's prepared for all the possible outcomes.

What They See: Draw three arrows on a piece of folded-over paper. The top arrow should be labeled "my line," the center arrow is labeled "base line," and the bottom arrow is labeled "your line."

Now pick any three objects to choose from and write out all three choices on coasters or napkins. You can pick "rock, paper, scissors," any three famous celebrities, or (as we did) just write down the first initials of any three people there (in our case, B, H, and M). Place all three choices in the row next to the "base line" arrow. Once the base line is set up, create two more sets of coasters and hand one to your volunteers and keep the other set for yourself.

"We're going to play a guessing game," you begin. "In a moment, I'm going to ask you to place your coasters in any order you want in your line. The only rule is that you can't place a coaster in a spot that matches what's already on the base line. Sound fair?"

"Oh, and to make sure you don't accuse me of doing anything sneaky, I'm going to make my selection first. I'll even place my coasters face-down so they don't affect your choices," you say. Once you've set your coasters in a row along "my line," have them make their decisions.

Stop everything: I'm going to spoil the end here, and say that your prediction is about to exactly match their choice. But how your prediction matches will depend on where they choose to lay out their coasters.

For starters, telling them that they can place the coasters in any configuration "as long as no coaster matches the base line," sounds like a fair setup, but in fact this limits them to only two possible outcomes. In our example, since the baseline was B H M, that means the only two possible outcomes were H M B, or M B H.

If they choose M B H: Reveal that you exactly predicted their choice by flipping over the coasters from "my line" and setting them on top of the coasters in the base line. You're left with an exact match, and there's no question that you predicted their choices!

If they choose H M B: Turn all three of the coasters in "my line" face up, saying, "Okay, here's what I chose for my line. And yet, before any of this started, I made this prediction." As you say this, unfold the piece of paper to reveal that along each of the

three lines, you've exactly predicted the position of all nine coasters!

Magicians call this having "multiple outs." By being prepared for both possibilities, you guarantee yourself an on-target prediction.

BLACK MAGIC

AUDIO COMMENTARY

bit.ly/1QanmNm

EPISODE

bit.ly/1OUm1MA

IMPRESSIVENESS: 3/5
★ ★ ★ ☆ ☆
CLASS: SECRET CODE
FACTORS: ANNOYS SUCKERS
REQUIRES: PARTNER, SECRET CODE

Both Black Magic and Sticks are so dead simple that both you and your friend can learn it in less than 30 seconds. Even better: you can perform these tricks all night long, and nobody will figure out the code.

Black Magic: "SWEET HOLY HOT SAUCE!" you shout out of nowhere. "Guys, you won't believe what just happened. Just this afternoon, Chad and I were walking down the street when KA-BLAM! We both just got struck by radioactive lightning."

"Crazy, right? So now we've got psychic powers. We'll even prove it to you; cover up Chad's face and ears and then choose any object in the room and point it out to me."

Skeptical, your friends reach over and point to the clock hanging across the room.

"CHAD!" you shout. "The object they selected . . . is it this fork?"

Chad shakes his head.

"What about this fan?"

"Nope," Chad replies.

"Hmm . . . this black table cloth?"

"That's not it," says Chad as he begins to lean back, interlacing his fingers behind his head.

"How about that clock?"

With a grin, Chad nods and says, "Yep. That's the one."

Your friends are more annoyed than amused. They accuse you of using some kind of hand motion to tip off your partner-in-crime. So you repeat the effect, this time with Chad's eyes covered the entire time.

Next, they accuse you of having a set pattern. "It's always the fifth object asked, isn't it?" they inquire. You respond by performing it again, and this time the correct object is the second one guessed.

"It's something in your voice, dude. You're using some kind of code word," they sneer. So you perform it again, this time without speaking a single word. You simply walk around and point to objects, until your partner exclaims "YES!" on the chosen item.

I'm not kidding here: you really could perform this all night. But if someone does figure it out, immediately bring him or her into the game. "HOLY COW! Did you see that? Jon just got struck by radioactive lightning as well!"

The Secret: It doesn't matter what you say. It doesn't matter how you look. It doesn't matter what kind of object is selected, because the dead-simple code behind Black Magic is . . .

The chosen object is always the one asked after you ask about a black object.

This is diabolical since you have an ever-shifting set of conditions each time you perform. By the time they start analyzing your actions, you've already sent the code!

Sticks: Similar to Black Magic, Sticks challenges your friends to crack a code. But in this case, you can perform the entire trick without a partner.

Grab a bunch of toothpicks, straws, or cocktail sticks. Toss them in the air, and very closely examine the random pattern they land in.

"Hmm . . . yup. This one is a three."

Toss them in the air again and take a look at the results. "Oh, wow! A six!"

Continue to toss the sticks like runes, each time carefully examining the results and giving a specific number. Answer any appropriate questions: Yes, there's a consistent reason for each number. No, you're not just making up numbers as you go along.

Remind them that once they solve the puzzle, the answer will always be obvious.

Chances are good that someone will crack the code after ten to twenty trials. When this happens, immediately become their best friend and bring them into the game. Remember that your job is to make this room a party, and nobody will be better off after some jerk loudly shouts the method behind your calculations.

Keep on playing until you just can't stand to leave them dangling on the hook any more; then reveal the truth:

The Secret: The pattern of the sticks, the number of sticks, the angles of the sticks . . . all are irrelevant. They are visual noise to draw attention away from the real cue: the number of fingers you've placed on the table as you lean forward to examine the sticks.

This one is nothing but misdirection. By making such a big deal out of tossing sticks, nobody thinks to look at such a minor detail like how many fingers you've placed on the table! Be subtle, be casual, and you'll be able to frustrate the hell out of them.

TRIPLE THREAT MIND-READING TRICK

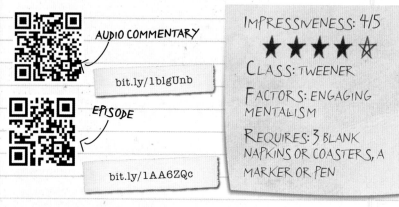

AUDIO COMMENTARY

bit.ly/1blgUnb

EPISODE

bit.ly/1AA6ZQc

This one's a blast. It's a fooler of a mind-reading trick, and you get to fully customize the routine to your friends' choices. Grab 3 coasters and a pen, and you're ready to go.

The Setup: Come up with any three things to choose from. The more personal you make the choices, the more fun this will be. For our demonstration, we came up with "Blondes," "Sexy Brunettes," and "Farm Animals."

Write down each choice on the blank side of a coaster and have your friend mentally select one of them. Make sure he remembers which position his choice is in as you turn all three coasters face-down.

"To make sure I have no idea which choice is where, I want you to swap the two coasters that aren't the one you chose while I look away," you say. Turning back around, say "Perfect. Now let's randomize it even more: start mixing the coasters around in a slow shuffle, three-card Monte style. Keep going as long as you like and stop any time you feel like they're totally mixed."

Once he stops shuffling, recap as you turn over all three coasters: "Remember: you kept your choice totally secret. You mixed up the cards before I even turned around, and then you mixed them up even more. Yet, I can tell that your secret choice was . . . Sexy Brunettes!"

The best part about this trick is that it's virtually unbustable. You can keep repeating it all night and never get caught on how it's done.

The Method: All you need to do is remember which choice was the middle coaster when you first turn away (we'll say it's "Farm Animals" in this example). When you turn back, just assume that it's still the same choice. When your friend starts doing the slow shuffle, follow the card you memorized the entire time. (Side note: If you're worried about losing the card in the shuffle, tell him only to "swap any two cards" as often as he likes. It'll do the same thing but be easier to follow.)

Once he finishes the shuffle, turn over the card you were following. You've been assuming it was still Farm Animals, but the reality of the card will tell you the choice they secretly made. There are only three possibilities:

1. **You turn over the card, and it's Farm Animals.** The exact card you thought you were following. This means that when you asked him to swap the two cards that weren't his choice, he left this one alone. Therefore, his secret choice was Farm Animals.

2. **You turn over the card, and it's Sexy Brunettes.** Since he swapped the cards he didn't choose, that means he didn't think of Sexy Brunettes, and he didn't think of Farm Animals. Therefore, his secret choice was Blondes.

3. **You turn over the card, and it's Blondes.** Following the same logic as in #2, he didn't choose Farm Animals or Blondes. Therefore, his secret choice was Sexy Brunettes.

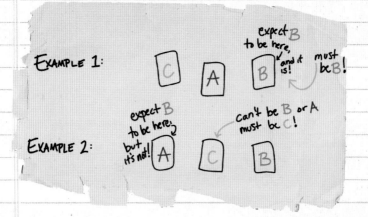

Just remember that if the followed card turns out to be what you expected, that's his secret choice. If it's not what you expected, then neither the card you're seeing nor the card you thought you were following are his choice.

Big thanks to my friend Seth Rovner of South Street Magic in Philadelphia for teaching this one to me.

QUICK HITS

AUDIO COMMENTARY

bit.ly/1yK6Eis

I get a LOT of suggestions for Scam School episodes, and many of them are awesome and clever . . . but just too short and direct to merit an entire 15-minute episode of their own.

So here I'm collecting 16 of my favorite short-and-simple bar tricks and challenges. Most are solid bar bets, but a few of them are a bit impractical for real-life use. Either way, you should be familiar with all of these. After all, how embarrassing would it be to get taken at your own bar? If you're going to dominate your home turf, you need to be familiar with all the bar tricks and challenges someone might throw at you.

Quick Hits:

#1: If you smoke, make this challenge to a friend: "I bet I can light this cigarette, take four deep drags on it, drop the ash, and the length will be exactly the same."

Answer all his questions: Yes, there will be smoke in each drag. Yes, you'll be dropping ash down. Yes, you'll really light the cigarette.

. . . and when he accepts the challenge: light the cigarette in the center. You'll be able to make good on your claim, and the cigarette will stay just as long after four drags.

#2: The Challenge: "I'm putting up this 20 bucks against a beer from you. All you need to do is jump over this 20 and land on the other side. I won't touch you, push you, or wrestle you, but in return, you can't touch or move the $20. Fair enough?"

The Scam: After the bet is secure, place the $20 snug in the corner of the room . . . he can't possibly jump over it and land on the other side!

#3: Pull out a penny and have your friend count the number of letters on the heads side of the coin. Odds are good that he'll come

up with 19 letters (20 if you count the "D" that may or may not appear under the date).

Ask if he's 100% sure . . . sure enough to bet a beer on it?

In fact, there are actually 22 or 23 letters, since clearly visible (albeit VERY small), are the letters "VDB" on Lincoln's bust (these are the initials of the engraver).

#4: I love this one. You've got two pieces: a bucket filled with a couple of matches, and a "tent" made from the unwrapped outer cover of a matchbox. The Challenge: get the tent over the matches without touching anything, and without leaving your seat.

You can't blow the tent over the bucket of matches without accidentally moving everything else around, and since you can't stand up, you can't move around to blow from the other side.

So instead, cup your hand just beyond the matches and blow into your hand, pushing the bucket of matches toward you, safely under the tent.

#5: Start with a simple 2x2 square made of matches. The Challenge: Cut the square into two, perfectly equal sides with exactly the same shape . . . using exactly 4 matches. All four matches must be used, and there can be no extraneous matches hanging loose.

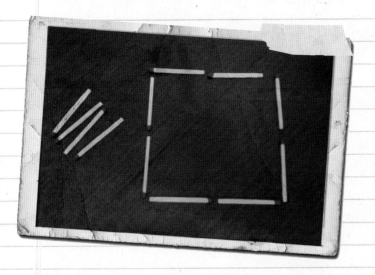

The Solution: there's not enough room for all 4 matches to directly bisect the square, so you need to use a zigzag pattern as shown in this photo . . .

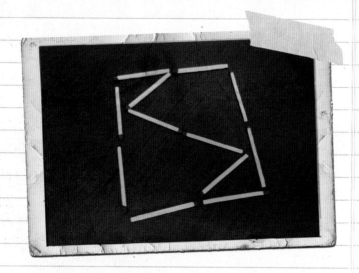

#6: Talent. It's so overrated.

Sure, there are highfalutin folks who can tie a cherry stem into a knot in their mouth . . . but what, are they better than you? Hell, no.

So how do you claim credit for oral talents you don't actually have? Pre-tie a cherry stem into a knot, and deposit it in the pocket between your gums and cheeks. It can sit there for a very long time without disturbing you, and you'll have it ready whenever you bring up the challenge.

Simply swap out the two stems, and you'll look as talented as any of those jerks!

#7: Not sure if this one's brilliant or just corny . . . Grab a dollar bill and challenge your friend to find as many heads as he can.

He'll spot George's head, of course. Oh, and the bald eagle has a head, too. And one would assume that the eye on the pyramid belongs to a head (though that's a stretch). Ugh . . . and if I have to hear one more person insist that there's a tiny owl in the webbing upper right-hand corner of the bill . . .

The answer to our challenge is much simpler: There are fifteen heads on a dollar bill. See if you can find them before reading the answer.

Give up? There's George's head, the eagle's head . . . and thirteen arrowheads.

#8: I don't care what you say. This one's adorable.

It's completely simple and a real visual treat. I first saw this in Diamond Jim Tyler's awesome book Bamboozlers:

Take a dollar bill and fold it down the center of George Washington's face, right through the center of his tight, stoic smile. Then make vertical folds in the reverse direction at the corners of his mouth.

Now hold the bill right in front of you, and tilt it up and down ... as you move the bill, George will appear to smile and frown.

#7: Offer your friend a simple challenge: he's going to roll a quarter down his forehead, off his nose, and hopefully have it land touching a target circle (which you've just drawn on a sheet of paper). If he can pull it off just two times in a row, you'll buy him a beer.

How can he resist? There's no downside, right?

Your real mission, however, is to make him look like a complete idiot. Each time he attempts the feat, you "mark" his result by using a pencil to draw a circle around the quarter. Allegedly this is to track his progress as he improves, but in reality you're using the pencil to coat the quarter in a ring of graphite. Each time he makes an attempt, he draws a big black line down the front of his face!

#8: Try this one with your friends to see if it works (and make sure you walk them through it verbally).

Add up the following column of numbers, all in your head:

When presented orally, this question causes a surprising number of people to come up with the answer "5,000." … Did it work on you?

```
 1000
   40
 1000
   30
 1000
   20
 1000
———————
NOT 5000 !
```

#9: And as long as we're dealing with numbers …

Quick! Write down (in numeric format) this number: "Eleven thousand eleven hundred and eleven."

… Did you come up with 11,1111? (If so, that would be "one hundred eleven thousand, one

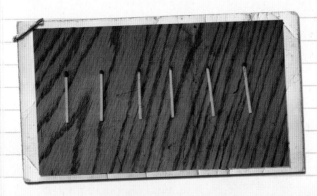

hundred eleven.) The right answer would be (oddly enough) "12,111."

#10: All right: one last number puzzle. Set up six matches or toothpicks just as you see here:

The challenge: use five additional matches to end up with exactly nine.

#11: Bite the heads off of 2 matchsticks, and arrange them in the

shape of a "T" (as shown here). The question: which stick is longer, the horizontal, or the vertical?

I always make sure to specifically phrase it as an either-or question. It causes most people to suspect a trick, so they'll respond with the smartass answer of "They're both the same!" In fact, the illusion is so strong that they'll be shocked to see how much longer the horizontal edge is than the vertical.

#12-#14: Always be on guard for simple wordplay tricks. They're cheesy and silly, but in rougher bars people will use them as a thinlyveiled excuses to extort cash from you. If you don't take the bet, you won't get threatened to pay up. Even jokingly accepting these bets can leave you dealing with threats and a hostile faceoff. This first one was actually tried on me in New Orleans several years ago:

"Nice shoes! I'll bet you five dollars I can tell you where you got 'em. I don't mean like what state or even what city. Bet me five dollars and I'll tell you exactly where you got those shoes."

And once you accept the bet, he says "Man, that's simple: you got 'em on your feet."

Maybe you'll run into a 7-foot-tall bruiser at the bar:

"Pfft. You think I'm strong? Son, you don't know the half of it. I'll bet you $20 that I can knock down that wall over there. ALL the way down. And I'll even bet that I won't break a sweat doing it."

"No way," you respond. "That's concrete and cinder block construction. I'll take that bet."

At which point, he calmly walks over to the wall and begins daintily knocking on it. First at the top, then knocking all the way down.

Perhaps someone makes an outrageous claim:

"Man, I'm the best in the world at balancing stuff. What, don't believe me? Hell, I'll betcha I can balance ten billiard balls on top of each other. I mean all in a straight line, too . . . straight up. And I won't be using no other special apparatus, neither. By the time I'm done settin' them up, there ain't gonna be nothing touching no balls, and they'll be in a stack 10 balls tall, hell, maybe 12, all in a straight line. If I'm wrong, you owe me a beer. Fair enough?"

Once he starts building his tower, it becomes painfully obvious that he's overstated his skills. He can't even stack two balls on top of each other.

"Well, hell. I guess I couldn't do it after all. But you agreed that 'if I'm wrong, you owe me a beer,' so I guess I'll be collecting it now."

#15: Word play bets can be cheesy and harmless, too. Try making your friend this promise:

"I can show you something that nobody in all of history has ever seen before, and something that nobody will ever see again."

Make good on your claim by cracking open a peanut. Explain that nobody has ever seen this inner nut. Then toss it in your mouth and chew it up, guaranteeing that nobody will ever see it again.

#16: Not much of a scam to this one, but it is a fun way to tease your friends. Fold a crease down the center of a five dollar bill and dangle it between your buddy's outstretched thumb and forefinger.

Tell him they can keep it, as long as they catch it in mid-air. It's got to be by reaction time only; they're not allowed to swoop their hand down to grab it as it descends. Oh, and there should probably be a $1 penalty for accidentally snatching the bill before you let go.

If you don't telegraph when you're about to let go, he won't

have a chance. His reaction time simply won't be fast enough, and

you'll probably come out ahead on his $1 penalties.

CELLAR DOOR